ROMAN
SPACES

ROMAN SPACES

ESSAYS AROUND AN EMPIRE

ERIC S. MORSE

IGUANA

Published by Iguana Books
720 Bathurst Street, Suite 303
Toronto, Ontario, Canada
M5V 2R4

Publisher: Greg Ioannou
Editor: Amanda Plyley
Front cover image: 'Replica Legionary Eagle standard of re-enactor unit *X Gemina*,' The Ermine Street Guard: 2014.
Front cover map: 'Germania,' published by Harper and Sons, New York, NY: 1849.
Front cover design: Eric S. Morse
Book layout design: Amanda Plyley

Library and Archives Canada Cataloguing in Publication

Morse, Eric S., 1949-, author
    Roman spaces : essays around an empire / Eric S. Morse.

Includes bibliographical references.
Issued in print and electronic formats.
ISBN 978-1-77180-087-7 (pbk.).--ISBN 978-1-77180-088-4 (bound).--
ISBN 978-1-77180-089-1 (epub).--ISBN 978-1-77180-090-7 (kindle).--
ISBN 978-1-77180-091-4 (pdf)

        1. Rome--Civilization. 2. Rome--History--Empire, 30 B.C.-476 A.D.
I. Title.

DG77.M67 2014   937'.06   C2014-907282-1
                                            C2014-907283-X

This is an original print edition of *Roman Spaces: Essays Around an Empire*.

Dedication

To Val Ross (1950-2008), littératrice, mentor and friend, who steered me gently into writing about issues, including Roman ones; to Mary Janigan and Morton Ritts, who braced my nerve through six years of lectures; to the Members of the Royal Canadian Military Institute in Toronto who have turned out staunchly to the lectures; to the friends and family who have put up with my Romanist obsession for years.

And with especial gratitude to

KATHRYN E LANGLEY HOPE

PATRONÆ LIBERALISSIMÆ OPTIMÆ MAXIMÆ
AMICÆ CARISSIMÆ

Dear friend, long-time patron and generous sponsor of this work.

Contents

Foreword

Those who know Eric Morse from his columns in the *Ottawa Citizen* or from his presentations at the Royal Canadian Military Institute will find in *Roman Spaces* the traits that make this *libellum* so engaging and well worth reading. Entertaining and endearingly irreverent on the one hand, pragmatic, probing, and learned on the other, Eric has a way of making his readers reconsider accepted wisdom or grand hypotheses built on questionable foundations. Unlike so many, he keeps his footing on the slender tightrope of reliable evidence. He disclaims any attempt at original scholarship, but here I put it to the reader that his essays serve an even more useful purpose—to look at the Roman past from fresh perspectives and, *mutatis mutandis*, compare the experience of that past with contemporary affairs. *Roman Spaces* is yet another reminder, in a day and age when the humanities seem to have gone badly astray, that the study of the classics retains its core value as the study of human nature. Character was destiny in the eyes of the ancients; and from Homer, to the Greek tragedians, to the Greek and Roman historians, to Vergil, and on through Plutarch, they sought to explain how human beings with their strengths and weaknesses, within their lights, surmounted or faltered before the constraints, limitations, imperfections, and pressures of this world.

It is odd and unfortunate that modern historians frequently make no place for people in their work, preferring instead to examine events, forces, or trends as though human beings and human agency have no role. Refreshingly, Eric's pieces become all the more worth reading for the attention he pays to the human factor and for the common sense he brings to his discussions. Speaking from my perspective as an old Byzantinist, I find the Byzantine world, with its self-fashioned, alluring image of order and stability, priding itself as being the very kingdom of heaven on Earth governed by God's regent, very much like the Roman world that can easily deceive us into thinking that the image of the *Pax romana* was the reality. It is Eric's approach to ask what in fact was possible, what was feasible, what was real or realistic behind the image. Numbers matter, time matters, geography matters, distances matter, and so does our recognition of the realm of information or choice available to the emperors, commanders, or politicians at a given moment.

Every essay in this book reads like a good conversation, true to the spirit of the Greek and Roman historians who wrote works to be read aloud, argued over, and enjoyed. And so it is a pleasure to extend a Latin invitation to readers: *tolle, lege, laetaberis*—*"pick up this book and read it, you'll be happy that you did."*

—*Dr. Eric McGeer, Toronto*

Introduction

That's the thing about the past, you can find anything you like there.

— *Dr. Margaret MacMillan, Munk Centre*
University of Toronto, March 24, 2014

It was just after the 1974 Canadian federal election that Prime Minister Pierre Elliott Trudeau, having said during the campaign that he would not bring in wage and price controls, did so. Instantly, Canadian pundits discovered the Roman Emperor Diocletian, who had brought in something that at least looked similar in 301 CE. There were editorials citing Diocletian's Edict on Maximum Prices as a sure guarantee that universalist remedies were doomed to failure.

In due course I encountered a book of essays, *Aspects of Antiquity*, by Dr. M. I. Finley, who explained gently that Diocletian was no ideologue but a simple military man and autocrat, that he was (as he himself says in the Preface to his Edict) upset that inflation was devaluing his soldiers' pay, and that when the solution obviously didn't work, he simply walked away from it a year or so later because he had not drunk any intellectual bathwater that would have committed him to sticking with a lost cause. Among other things, he didn't have to face an election campaign.

Trudeau's anti-inflation measures lasted four years, were intended as a temporary measure, were far more limited in scope, and may have helped him to lose the 1979 election. The only really useful takeaways from Diocletian are: (1) what a miracle of organization it was that with fourth-century administrative technology and communications, the Imperial bureaucracy was able to compile so comprehensive and accurate a table of values for just about everything available in the Empire, and (2) how dangerous it is to pull historical comparisons out of a hat.[1]

This book, which is based on a series of lectures given to the Royal Canadian Military Institute between 2008 and 2014 and dedicated to the late Canadian littératrice and commentator Val Ross, attempts something of the reverse. Its key chapters attempt to look at the Romans' position in their world through the lens, gingerly applied, of modern geopolitics and in particular of the lessons we are now trying to learn from the past decade, when it has become clear that the global universe of a hundred and ninety-three sovereign players and heaven knows how many 'others' is a far more complex and fragmented power structure than the old bipolar world was, or than we ever imagined.

In its way this is as dangerous as attempting to draw lessons from history, since (as Finley also points out) the

---

[1] Self-help management pieces on a vaguely Roman theme keep popping up in popular business media. My personal favourite is still *Management Secrets of Attila the Hun*. As I write this, Twitter touts a piece called *Lessons from Great Armies of Ancient Rome*—whose track record was at best uneven. I'm waiting for *Lie, Cheat and Embezzle like Servilius Caepio*...but perhaps Colleen McCullough has covered that ground well enough.

worldview and attitudes of Classical society were 'desperately alien' to ours. However, our own age is becoming increasingly aware that societies coexist within this era that are as desperately alien to each other as our Roman spiritual ancestors are to us in the West. Modern international relations studies attempt to bridge these gulfs and it is probably no bad thing to try it with a society that has ceased to exist but still endlessly fascinates—and, through no fault of its own, misleads.

To offer a single example, there is no agreement on how the Romans viewed geographic space. Did they understand large-scale maps and could they think in terms of geopolitical relationships, or, based on their surviving travel itineraries, was their perception strictly linear?

Possibly, it was both. There was a three-dimensional map of the City mounted by Septimius Severus in Rome for all to see. On the other hand, large-scale maps drawn any time up to about 1500 CE were grotesquely inaccurate from a modern perspective. Still, they conveyed a sense of spatial relationship, even if distorted.

Consider how different a Millennial's spatial perception, formed by Google Earth and GPS navigation systems, is from a Boomer's, formed by National Geographic maps and the Oxford World Atlas. At the simplest level, people who drive a car view geography vastly differently from people who do not. Yet we coexist.

The historian Dio Cassius may or may not have thought geopolitically (or in terms of maps) but he knew Imperial overexpansion when he saw it. Tacitus may not have had a cartographer's view of Greater Germany but he certainly had a good idea of what and who was 'out there' for a very long way, and—more to the point—so did the Imperial generals on the frontiers. What threats might be coming at them, or what somebody 'out there' intended to do, on the other hand, is a conundrum that modern security agencies with all their technology have not solved. The highest-resolution photographs may give an idea of what's there but they cannot tell you what it will do five minutes from now.[2] We cannot read the minds of opponents, no more could the Romans.

Likewise, the technology of intelligence acquisition has not changed the dynamics of its interpretation and translation into policy one iota. We are able to make mistakes more quickly now. The President of the United States has exactly as many hours in his day as the Emperor of Rome did, and far too much, and too unreliable, information coming at him. Marcus Aurelius had too little: he had to deal with an information lag of about seven days between the Army of the Upper Danube and Rome—which is why Marcus Aurelius ended up spending most of his reign 'in theatre'. Barack Obama can sit and watch an assassination on the other side of the world, but he can have no clue what might be coming at him from another direction because it's being delayed, filtered through contending bureaucracies, and in any case

---

[2] The deception campaign waged by Russia in East Ukraine in mid-2014 is a perfect example of this.

the Administration's mind is elsewhere.[3] Relative attention spans in Rome and Washington are not much different. The fog of war has changed in shape but not in nature.

Rome did not quite have to deal with a 193-player universe, and Rome only ever had one other state with whom it had to deal as an equal (Parthia/Persia; Chapter Three). But broken down into what the Governors on the frontiers had to deal with—and the Emperor was forced to delegate them maximum latitude consonant with regime preservation—there might have been nearly that many shades of relationship with bordering peoples from Britain to Arabia via the Crimea and the Caucasus and back around to Gibraltar. Modern relationships are global and multiplex. Roman relationships were more linear, geographically shallower, but no less nuanced.

In the year of the first Val Ross lecture in 2008, palaeontologists in Manitoba had just discovered a new species of mosasaur, a sea-going reptile. That is, they discovered two teeth and a piece of jawbone. This

[3] Former US Secretary of Defense Robert Gates in his memoir *Duty* refers to the difficulty of making sensible national security decisions based on incomplete information provided to a group of at most eight perpetually exhausted people. I recall a famous instance in 1976 when the world's foreign ministries were caught flat-footed by the African boycott of the Montreal Olympics because attention was focussed on Canada's refusal to let Taiwan compete in the face of Chinese protests.

resembles the experience of the Romanist.[4] Classical scholarship, with its roots in philology, has mined a very difficult vein very thoroughly. What is left to us of classical literature is not likely to expand except perhaps through very lucky archaeological breaks.

Classical scholarship began to broaden into interdisciplinary approaches before World War II; 1939 was a seminal year. That is when Ronald Syme's *The Roman Revolution* first applied the concepts and methodology of political science to the Age of Augustus. In so doing, Syme forced no comparisons with political dynamics and regimes of his day, but he forced historians to adopt a more analytical and interdisciplinary view of classical history.

Thanks to applied technology, archaeology is advancing hugely, but it tells a different, harder to interpret, more granular tale. The find (still continuing) of the commandant's archives and assorted other correspondence at Vindolanda in northern England in 1973 has given us a wealth of detail, some of it not easily understood, and has vastly expanded our knowledge of Roman writing methods. The find of three battlefields in Germany has added dimensions to our knowledge and led to drastic reassessments of Roman capabilities. We are unlikely ever to find

---

[4] As of June 2014, German archaeologists have discovered a Roman marching camp as far into Germany as the Battle at the Harzhorn described in Chapter Six. But all they can say, lacking thus far any coins or identifiable artifacts, is that it might have been built any time between the first and third centuries CE.

anything so precious as Trajan's Dacian War Diaries or the lost military manuals of Frontinus. But there was far more to 'Roman space' than anyone before the twenty-first century imagined.

As this book is written the post–Cold War international order seems to be coming apart at the seams. We—and the Romans—were brought up in a tradition of thinking that there was a Law of Nations, that wars lasted a season and battles were decisive, that there were bad guys and good guys, and that the *pax*, once imposed, was eternal.

It wasn't that way for them either.

———

The original lectures on which these essays are based have been, in the best tradition of Cicero and his friends, revised for reading, and include many of the 'good parts' that original time limits left out. Chapter Three has been written for this book. Chapter Eight is an expansion of an article published in *Sitrep*, the journal of the Royal Canadian Military Institute, and of an earlier piece in the *Ottawa Citizen*.

The book contains no original scholarship; what interpretations it may advance are the author's responsibility alone. There are plenty of footnotes, almost all of them in the 'colour commentary' category. There is a readers' guide for those who want to explore more deeply.

Welcome to *Roman Spaces*.

Toronto, Ontario, 2014

Hadrian's Wall

Eboracum
(York)

Varus
Disaster
x 9 CE

BRITAIN

x

Londinium
(London)

LOWER
GERMANY

Battle at the
Harzhorn,
235 CE

Moguntiacum
(Mainz)

UPPER GERMANY
AND RAETIA

GAUL

Mutina 43 BCE
x

SPAIN

Rome
(Roma)

Carthage
(Carthago)

PROCONSULAR
AFRICA

0   200   400   600   800   1000 km

THE ROMAN EMPIRE 125 CE

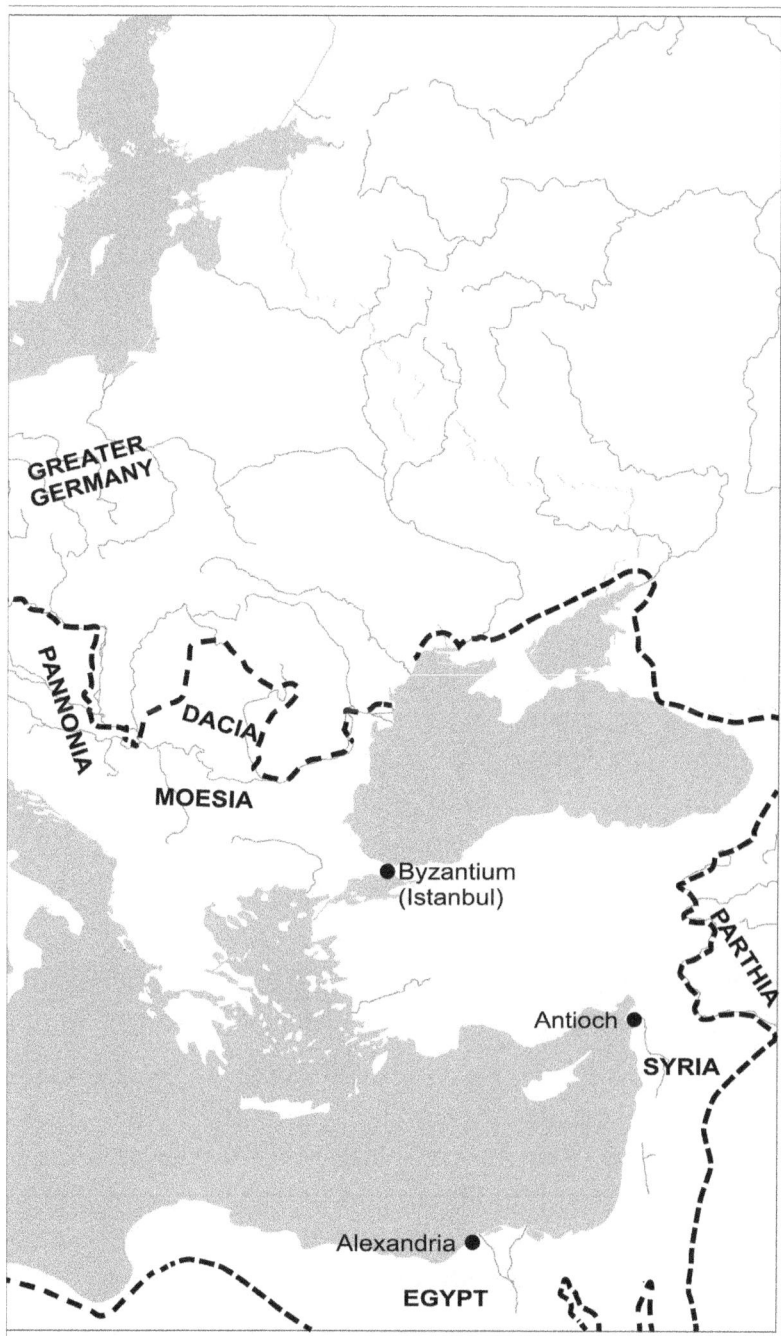

Chapter One

From Our Special Correspondent: A Battlefield Dispatch

A really good day's work.

— *S. Sulpicius Galba, April 15, 43 BCE*

There once was a man named Servius Sulpicius Galba. Actually, there once were a lot of men named Servius Sulpicius Galba, but only one per generation; the Roman high aristocracy wasn't all that creative when it came to naming first-born sons, and you didn't get a clan much higher in the aristocracy than the *gens Sulpicia*. The first one we know of shows up in mid–third century BCE, probably born during the First War with Carthage, otherwise known as the First Punic War. His grandson was a consul and dictator during the war with Hannibal (the Second War with Carthage), and Rome was never without one of them thereafter until the last one became *Empéreur-du-jour* in the very turbulent year of 69 CE and earned the one-liner from Tacitus, "Everyone agreed that he was capable of ruling—if he'd never ruled."

The Galba that we're interested in was that brief Emperor's great-grandfather, born sometime around 90 BCE. He was a supporter of Julius Caesar's, and served with him in Gaul in the 50s where he commanded the

Twelfth Legion and lost a battle against the locals in 57. He was nominated Praetor in 54 by the Caesarean faction, but he seems to have gotten involved with the Ides of March conspiracy in 44, possibly because Caesar wouldn't nominate him for consul, and also allegedly because Caesar had had an affair with Galba's wife, Postumia, which would make her neither the first nor the last to be so honoured.

What he did that makes him interesting—and it makes him *very* interesting—was write the first morning-after, first-person general officer's account of a battle that we have in history, and the only reason we have it is that he wrote it to his colleague, the orator Cicero, and it wound up in Cicero's collected correspondence. As it happens, Galba was hell with a pen, and his account is one of the crispest pieces of military journalism ever written. It is also the only account of its kind that we have from the entire classical period.

Literature in any language doesn't have much by way of military correspondence or memoirs until about the end of the seventeenth century, and it doesn't really get going until the Napoleonic Wars. It's not hard to see why. The late eighteenth century saw the first emergence of a literate mass society that was hungry to read and an industry and economy that could feed the hunger.

The business model for the Internet café[1] emerged during that period. The London papers cost a penny or

---

[1] Tom Standage of *The Economist* is deeply fascinated by previous iterations of social phenomena. His most recent book, *The Writing on the Wall*, is a survey of social media beginning with the Romans' use of

two each. Most villagers couldn't afford that and in most villages only one or two people could read anyway—possibly the curate and the doctor or the schoolmaster if the village had one. But once there were papers, people wanted to know what they said. (It's not so much that 'information wants to be free' as that 'people want to know'.) The pub owners figured the game out early. The local publican would subscribe to the papers, which would be tossed onto the stagecoach in London and dropped off at destinations. Since the stagecoach was a scheduled run, everybody would show up at the pub when it was due, order a beer, and listen while the local literate resident read the papers out loud. Then they'd have a fight and everybody would go home happy.

By 1803 Admiral Lord Nelson had become the first true media celebrity. After that there was no holding back the

---

graffiti-as-Twitter. He published it on the 'Publish like Cicero' model (give a copy to all your friends and hope they'll copy it and pass it on). Unfortunately for the working stiff, 'Publish like Cicero' equals 'Publish like the Huffington Post', which is one of the many reasons we have so little left from an astonishingly prolific Classical publishing industry. Publishing was a game only the rich could play. It is also one of the reasons so much of Classical writing is very hard-to-get for us moderns: they were writing for each other, they assumed (as people of all ages do) mutual comprehensibility of context, and what they wanted to read and why they wanted to read it is sometimes now none too clear. The outstanding (and superbly readable) classical historian M. I. Finley summarizes the problem with his essay 'Desperately Alien' in *Aspects of Antiquity*.

flood, and military memoirs and correspondence became a real literary genre.

But before about 1600, almost nothing. We can practically name what exists on the fingers of one hand:

Xenophon's *March Up-country (Anabasis)* discusses how a group of Greek mercenaries around 400 BCE escaped from total disaster in the heart of the Persian Empire and managed to get home in one piece.

As political propaganda, Caesar's *Commentary on the Gallic War* is masterly and it isn't bad history either. It set a standard for Latin readable by moderns (which Galba actually approaches).

In the first chapter or two of Josephus' *Jewish War*, he describes his own combat role in the Jewish rebellion, but that was written after considerable time for reflection and getting his political attitude readjusted in the comfort of a Roman townhouse (*'He defected, you know'*).

Once you've read *Agricola* by Tacitus, you realize what a pity it is that the old general didn't write his own story of three remarkable postings in Britain. He fought the rebel queen Boudicca as a young Tribune under Suetonius Paulinus in 61 CE. He commanded the Twentieth Legion right after the great civil wars of 69-70; a tough time to hold a command in Britain. He commanded the Army of Britain at Mons Graupius in 83 against the wild Caledonian boys. But he never wrote about any of it himself, probably wisely in the political circumstances. The *Agricola* is a distillation of what Tacitus would have heard over many dinners at his father-in-law's place, and it has a definite political axe to grind that the old man may or may not have shared.

Arrian's *Order of Battle Against the Alani* almost qualifies. Arrian was a friend of the Emperor Hadrian (117-138 CE), a military historian, and the Governor of the province of Cappadocia (eastern Turkey) when a tribe called the Alani (the Ossetians of the North Caucasus claim to be their descendants), who specialized in heavy cavalry, invaded it. Arrian wrote about his force deployment in great detail; he'd apparently never had the chance to play with real legions before and was very proud of it. It's very informative[2] but it isn't a narrative and wasn't meant to be. If he'd kept writing about what happened after the deployment itself, it could have been a hit. But apparently Arrian didn't think it was all that interesting. And we don't know for certain that it even ended in a battle.

Ammianus Marcellinus in his *Roman History* has a harrowing tale of his escape with two friends from the siege of Amida on the Persian frontier in 359 CE and his time 'inside' during the siege. First person, but with time to reflect and do some massaging. By that time losing a battle to the Persians was no longer unmentionable and Ammianus tells a first-class story.[3]

And finally, twelve hundred years later, Bernal Diaz del Castillo's *Conquest of Mexico*, written by one of the small band of conquistadors who went with Cortez and conquered the Aztec Empire. Diaz wrote a brilliant eyewitness narrative based on his own experiences and

---

[2] But a little obscure because he insists on using Greek terms to describe a Latin-speaking army with no agreed conversion lexicon.

[3] All of these works, along with Cicero, are available either in print editions or (for free!) over the World Wide Web.

interviews with fellow soldiers—a pioneering format that almost anticipates early twentieth century styles of journalism—but he wrote it in the 1550s and it never saw the light of day until the manuscript was discovered in 1632, thirty-five years after he died. Which again proves the point about markets.

There may be a very few others, but those are the big ones before the eighteenth century. And then there is Galba, preserved in Cicero's *Letters to His Friends*, Book Ten, Letter Thirty. In Galba's case (and many others' in the collection), it is a letter from a friend, which Cicero may have considered politically significant, or it may simply have struck him as a great read, which it is.

There's no reason why other Romans shouldn't have written after-battle letters and plenty of reason to think that quite a few of them did, but nothing else has survived. Any of the generals who wrote good tactical handbooks could have written good memoirs, and even a few centurions could have wielded a pen if they'd felt like it. But the market simply wasn't there in the day, it would have been politically very dangerous (several historians have done some heavy skating around events in their recent past, and Ammianus gets away with an amazing amount of candour), and what we have left of classical letters in any case is a drop in the bucket, often preserved by pure chance.[4]

---

[4] *The Swerve: How the World Became Modern* by Stephen Greenblatt is—among other things—a marvellous account of ancient publishing, how its output was lost, and how some of it was rediscovered by several dedicated manuscript-hunters in the fifteenth century.

There is a curious link from the eighteenth century to classical Rome. Before he died, Julius Caesar founded the *Daily Gazette (Acta Diurna)*, a sort of cross between the *Canada Gazette* and *Hansard*, that summarized public notices and the proceedings of the Senate, and was posted up on boards in the Forum. It probably wasn't a year before it started accepting paid advertising, mostly wedding announcements and social notices. If somebody can write it, somebody else wants to read it, and the aristocracy used to send their slaves to the Forum every day to copy down the hot stuff. But the market wasn't what you'd call viral. Eighteenth-century England's market was.

There is one more reference that illustrates the utterly random factor of preservation. We have *one line* from the second century that has driven modern scholars mad with frustration. It's in a Latin grammar book published around 500 CE, and it reads: *We then advanced to Berzobim, next to Aizi.* That's it. '*Inde Berzobim, deinde Aizi, processimus*'. Preserved as an example of good syntax, no more, no less. It seems to be the sole surviving fragment of the *Dacica*, the Dacian War Commentaries of the Emperor Trajan published around 110 CE, which if intact might rival the War Diaries of the *Oberkommando der Wehrmacht* as a contemporary historical document, and would certainly tell us things we can only guess about the history depicted in sculpture on Trajan's Column in Rome. We even know where Berzobim and Aizi are. But the book is gone, probably forever.

So Galba wins the literary jackpot, and no matter what else he did or didn't do in his life, that one letter entitles him to a place in history. It's a great letter. Four hundred and twenty-nine words in Latin, about six hundred and twenty-five in English translation—just the right length for a newspaper column. It describes one of the most confusing battles in history, because the political situation that led to it was so completely out of hand that quite probably none of the players at the time understood what they were doing or why they were doing it, with one possible exception.

The time was April, 43 BCE. The place was an embanked stretch of the Aemilian Way in northern Italy, in a marshy spot between Mutina and Bononia, the modern Modena and Bologna. The players were Decimus Brutus (but not *that* Brutus, *his* name was Marcus), the Consuls for the year 43 Aulus Hirtius and Gaius Vibius Pansa, the ex-consul for 44 Mark Antony, and an ambitious, vicious, and sneaky nineteen-year-old kid sporting the name of Caesar, who was never, ever referred to back then as Octavian—at least not where he could hear it.

Julius Caesar was assassinated on March 15, 44 BCE. (Calpurnia said, *Julie don't go, but would he listen?*[5]) The fact that the assassins were all close associates of his made things hideously confusing. The fact that everybody in Rome, bloody-handed or not, was somehow beholden to Caesar, and that none of the

---

[5] Johnny Wayne and Frank Shuster's "Rinse the Blood Off My Toga" first aired on *The Ed Sullivan Show*, May 2, 1958. It is, of course, an authoritative account of the whole ghastly day. And it's on YouTube.

assassins seems to have had any idea what to do next, made things even messier. The fact that Antony got wind of the plot, tried to warn Caesar, was outsmarted, and then before they'd even rinsed the blood off the togas, passed an amnesty through the Senate (literally the day after) simply added insult to injury.

It became immediately clear that the Roman Street and especially Caesar's veterans did not like the amnesty. Things became rambunctious. It became clear that any of the assassins who wanted to remain healthy had better leave town fast, so in the course of negotiations among (a) the conspirators, (b) Antony (the surviving Consul for 44), (c) Hirtius and Pansa (the two Consuls-elect for 43), and (d) just about anybody else in town who could toss in a stake, most of the principal conspirators were given hasty appointments well out of Rome. That would include Marcus Brutus and Lucius Cassius who both went east and began raising troops for a civil war against any comers. Decimus Brutus got Cisalpine Gaul (northern Italy) from which, if he could get enough troops together, he could threaten whatever happened to be calling itself the government in Rome on any given day.

The reason that most people who were educated in English know very little about any of this is that it's one of the highly confusing parts that Shakespeare left out.[6]

Antony was trying hard to be supreme leader of the Caesarean faction. He had already dipped his fingers

---

[6] HBO's *Rome* did not leave it out.

into Caesar's personal funds (which in any case were getting a little muddled up with the Treasury), he was attempting to reconstitute Caesarean veteran formations, and he had managed to get the major assassins out of the city.

He was having a bad time with Cicero, mainly over Cicero's anger that Antony wasn't fulfilling the public terms of Caesar's will, when all of a sudden in early May 44 a wild card showed up from overseas.

Caesar's 18-year-old great-nephew Octavian had been a junior officer with the Parthia expeditionary force then ramping up across the Adriatic (to avenge Caesar's political partner Crassus: see Chapter Three) when he got the news. He and a few close pals moved fast. On landing in Italy on May 1, 44, he got further news that he was Julius Caesar's principal heir in name and in fortune. He promptly took the name and tried to take the fortune. When he couldn't get his hands on the money because Antony wouldn't let go, he began borrowing enough to build a strong private force of Caesar's veterans.

Obviously, this was not going to end well.

Antony by now was feeling some major heat of his own for having been too accommodating to the conspirators. Cicero spotted an opening, moved in, and by autumn 44 had teamed up with Octavian to deliver a vicious series of speeches against Antony (the *Philippics*) which Antony never forgave or forgot.

By November, Antony's relations with the Senate were strained enough that he was handed a command in northern Italy—as replacement for Decimus Brutus, effective January 1, 43—and headed north with at least two legions, planning to pick up two more of Caesar's veteran units en route. Octavian pulled a fast one and grabbed the pair while Antony wasn't looking. With those behind him he had no trouble at all persuading the Senate to admit him to its ranks (he had had no legal standing at all before then) and legitimizing his command of them as a sort of freelance deputy to Consuls Hirtius and Pansa.

In the meantime Antony had taken up his northern Italy command and was besieging Brutus, who refused to quit, in Mutina. Brutus' forces were bottled up, probably starving, and he played no active role in what came later. Meanwhile in Rome, Octavian, Hirtius, and Pansa, with Cicero cheering enthusiastically in the background, had managed to get Antony declared a public enemy.

In late winter Hirtius and Octavian took a force of about four veteran legions including the two Caesarian units that Octavian had snaffled (one of which was called *Martia*, but its number is nowhere recorded)[7] and headed north to deal with Antony. Pansa followed, with four legions of recruits.

---

[7] Much more about names and numbers of legions in Chapter Four.

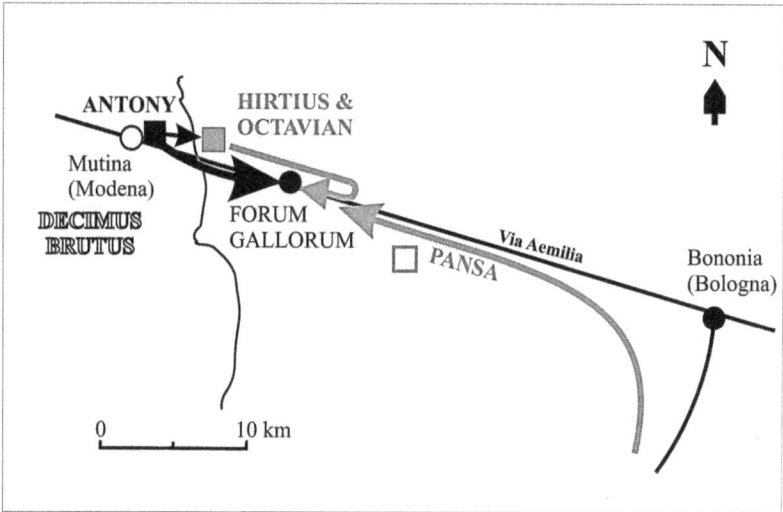

Dispositions around Mutina, April 43 BCE, after Lawrence Keppie

By early April the scene around Mutina looked like this (*Figure 1*). There were effectively four forces in the field: Decimus Brutus holed up in Mutina and in no shape for action, Antony based just east of him (the black square) astride the Via Aemilia, Hirtius and Octavian camped just east of *him* (the grey square next to the black square), and Pansa coming up through Bononia with four legions of recruits and making a final marching camp (the hollow grey square) just east of the village of Forum Gallorum on the evening of the 13th. Our man Galba was with Hirtius and Octavian, at least nominally commanding the *Martia*—except that on the day of the battle, he wasn't.

There were two actions in the campaign: the encounter at Forum Gallorum on April 14, which is the one that Galba's letter describes, and the one at Mutina itself on April 21. Both were severe defeats for Antony, although the action of April 14 was nearly a disaster for the consuls—Galba's letter does not really make clear how near-run it was, probably because it was written the morning after, by which time it was clear that they'd won, so why waste ink on the embarrassing bits? He might not have even had a grasp of the real casualty count by then.

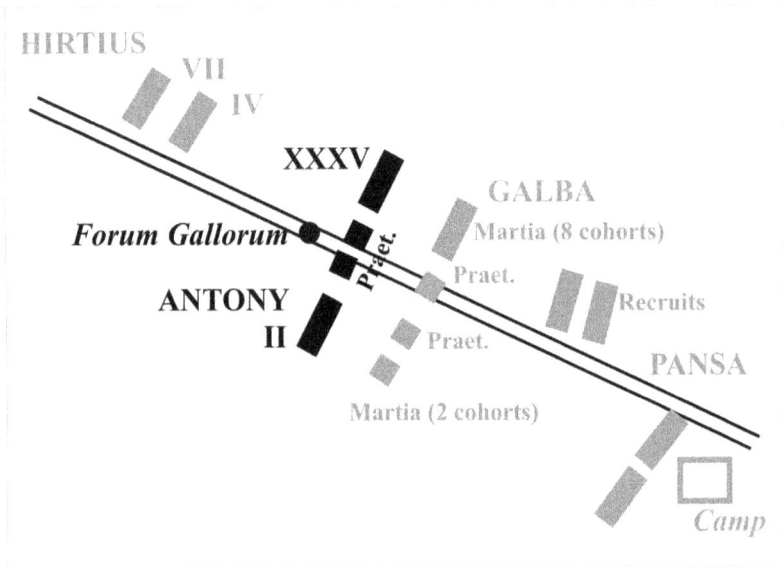

The action of April 14 at Forum Gallorum, after Lawrence Keppie

If you look at the battle graphic (*Figure 2*) for April 14, it looks as if Antony was caught in a meat grinder, and in fact in the end Antony *was* caught in a meat grinder, but the graphic depicts a sequence of events over about 14 hours from morning until late at night. It wasn't a foregone conclusion in the morning, and the first engagement in marshy land on either side of the causeway—so that neither flank could see what the other was doing—went very badly for Pansa's forces. It would have gone far worse without some very proactive thinking by Hirtius on the night of April 13.

One thing to note about the letter itself is what it doesn't say about Galba's own role in the battle, which probably at least started out as 'designated floater'. Galba, as he admits, was on detached duty to Pansa's element coming up from the south. In fact he was acting as a high-ranking bicycle courier, he was out of a line command, and he was seriously unhappy about it. He manages to leave out the name of the officer— Decimus Carfulenus—who actually commanded the *Martia* that morning. That's not surprising since Carfulenus was one of Octavian's henchmen, may actually have been the agent who talked *Martia* into defecting, and moreover seems to have gotten himself killed in action sometime during the day. Galba possibly assumed command of the unit thereafter. But whoever was in charge of *Martia* in the action, if Hirtius had not sent Carfulenus out with them the night before to reinforce Pansa's recruits, Antony's veterans would have wiped the floor with the recruits. Our only other source for the day's events—the historian Appian, writing two hundred years later (which means he was writing now about events in 1812 with fewer sources)—mentions Carfulenus. He is also far more explicit about casualties.

Casualties on both sides were appalling. By the end of the day Antony and Pansa are said to have each lost about half their shock troops, and Octavian's Praetorian cohort[8] was wiped out. The veterans in *Martia* are said to have warned Pansa's recruit units not to engage if they did make it onto the field in time because they'd only get in the way, which is very interesting in itself since it underscores how big a difference experience made in an infantry shock action.

It wasn't the first time Roman professional troops in a civil war had refused point-blank to back down from each other, and it certainly wasn't the last. Accounts agree that they sank their teeth into each other like pit bulls. Galba notes high casualties but doesn't stress them; again, it was the morning after victory and, having been through Gaul and the war against Pompey, he was presumably fairly blasé about high body counts.

The two actions at Mutina made Octavian's political career. Pansa was mortally wounded in the action of April 14 (Galba may also not have realized this when he wrote) and Hirtius was killed in that of April 21. That left the Senate without consuls, Antony without an effective army, the Ides of March conspirators loose in the East, and Octavian in the catbird seat. He formed the Second Triumvirate with Antony and with Lepidus who was a lightweight but had ambitions, money, and troops close to Rome. They instituted the mass proscriptions of late 43, and by the end of the year, as one modern historian

---

[8] Every senior general had a Praetorian bodyguard cohort at that point, a picked force. The Imperial Praetorian Guard came along later, but the old commanders' bodyguard units were the Republican precedent that Augustus Caesar used to create it.

has put it, everybody mentioned in the letter except Octavian and Antony wound up 'spectacularly dead'.

And so, the letter. Four hundred and twenty-nine words of crunchy Latin, a bit over six hundred in colloquial English. Just a little bit self-centred, slightly blurred by the fog of war, and as crisp a column as Reuters ever filed.

From Servius Sulpicius Galba, to Marcus Tullius Cicero:

On April 14, the day Pansa was due to reach Hirtius' camp, I was with him because I had been sent forward a hundred miles to make contact and tell him to hurry things up. That day Antony led out two legions for battle, the Second and the Thirty-Fifth, and two Praetorian cohorts, his own and Silanus'—plus elements of the veteran reserve.

He came out to meet us because he thought we only had the four legions of recruits. But, under cover of night, to make our arrival in the camp less risky, Hirtius had sent us support in the form of the Legio Martia*—which I usually commanded— and two Praetorian cohorts.*

When Antony's cavalry made their appearance, neither the Martia *nor the Praetorians could be kept in check and we were forced to follow them, since we couldn't hold them back. Antony had his main force at Forum Gallorum, and wanted to hide the fact that he had legions present: he only let us see his cavalry and light infantry. When Pansa saw that the legion was advancing without orders, he ordered two legions of recruits to follow them. After we had got across a narrow strip of marsh and woodland, we formed a line twelve cohorts long.*

The two legions of recruits had not yet appeared on the scene. Suddenly Antony brought his two legions out of the village, formed line, and charged immediately. At first the fighting was so intense that neither side could have fought harder; even so, the right wing, where I was stationed with eight cohorts of the Martia, *drove back Antony's Thirty-Fifth at the first shock, so that we advanced more than half a mile beyond our original position. At this point Antony's cavalry looked like outflanking our right, so I began to pull back and to throw our light infantry into battle against their Moorish horse, to keep them from attacking our rear.*

Meanwhile I saw that I was in among Antony's troops, and that Antony himself was actually some way behind me. I immediately threw my shield away and galloped in the direction of a legion of recruits that was coming up from the camp. The Antonians gave chase. Our people looked like they were going to throw their pila.⁹ I don't know what fate saved me but they recognized me at the last minute.

On the main road itself, where Octavian's Praetorian cohort was, the fighting lasted a long time. The left wing, which was weaker, having only two cohorts of the Martia *and a Praetorian cohort, began to pull back because they were being flanked by the cavalry, in which Antony is extremely strong. When all our formations had withdrawn, I began to retreat, the last of all, towards our camp.*

Antony, thinking he had it won, believed he could now take the camp, but when he got there he took heavy losses without accomplishing anything at all. By now Hirtius had heard what was happening. He took twenty veteran cohorts (i.e., the

---

⁹ *Pilum*, plural *pila*: the standard Roman infantry javelin.

Fourth and Seventh Legions—Keppie), and counterattacked Antony as he was returning to his camp. He destroyed Antony's forces and put him to flight on the very spot where the main battle had been, at Forum Gallorum. About 10 p.m. Antony got back to his own camp at Mutina with only his cavalry intact. Hirtius now proceeded to the camp where Pansa's two other legions had endured Antony's attack. So Antony lost the majority of his experienced forces. However this was not possible without some losses in our Praetorian cohorts and the Martia. *Two eagles and sixty standards—all Antony's—were captured. A really good day's work.*

Written from the camp, April 15th.[10]

---

[10] The text of the letter is an adaptation of Lawrence Keppie's translation in *The Making of the Roman Army*, 1984, checked against the original Latin text.

Chapter Two

All This Without a War College:
Policy by the Seat of Your Tunic

The general must neither be so undecided that he entirely distrusts himself nor so stubborn as to think that nobody can have a better idea…for such a man is bound to make costly mistakes.

— Onasander, The General, about 50 CE

In 1745, two British Colonels trying to plan the occupation of the Scottish Highlands could (and did) ask themselves, "What did Agricola do when he was here?" They may have been fooling themselves a little; in 1745 archaeology was barely beginning and they might have had trouble telling an Agricolan fort from an ambitious farmstead. But they were at least asking the right questions.

In 83 CE Governor Julius Agricola had had three British postings, a highly experienced command cadre, and centuries of conventional and unconventional warfighting *lore* behind him, but as far as the particular operational circumstances went, he had no one to ask but himself.

Roman policy-making was conservative, incrementally innovative, improvisational, but never sophisticated. Romans didn't have the precedents that their Western cultural descendants have (and too often abuse and/or ignore). They *were* the precedents.

History does not proceed logically except in hindsight. We retroject familiar patterns from our own experience, in the very human hope of creating order from the chaos of the past. So, though it may well be that the Late Imperial Roman Army evolved logically out of the Early Imperial Roman Army, which in turn evolved logically out of the Army of the Late Roman Republic, there was nothing planned or foreordained about any of it. Nobody in the court of Constantine the Great brought out a Defence White Paper that said: *There is a need for a separate field army and frontier army from now on, and these big old infantry legions are so second century, let's split them up and introduce a bunch of tiny new ones and by the way, it's all mobile defence in depth from here on in.*

In the early 1970s the American strategic thinker Edward Luttwak decided to try his hand at defining the grand strategy of the Roman Empire.[1] He based his assessment on the knowledge that between the third and fourth centuries, there was a movement away from linear frontier defences, toward a practice of fortifying settlements and strongpoints far deeper behind the frontier, and garrisoning troops in cities well behind the frontiers. He also knew that in the fourth century, there were field armies with major cavalry components which were at the immediate disposition of the

---

[1] In a book called, not unreasonably, *The Grand Strategy of the Roman Empire* (1975). One of the book's more problematic issues is that no one has ever satisfactorily defined 'grand strategy'.

Emperors or their regional field marshals. From these two historical bases a theory grew, really culminating in Luttwak's effort, that the Late Roman Empire adopted a strategy of 'defence-in-depth', employing mobile reserve forces in place of an Early Imperial strategy of 'preclusive defence'.

The Romans themselves had no body of theory that could have defined a grand strategy; Roman organizational solutions were reactive, intuitive, and conservative. There were practical concerns; no matter how much cavalry you add to a field army, these are not motorized regiments. Roman cavalry never exceeded thirty miles a day on a good road, and the infantry not over twenty. The concept of a deep 'mobile reserve' over Imperial distances thus becomes meaningless.[2] Reserves they may have been; mobile they were not.[3] The Army of the early Empire was probably just as effective at deploying to trouble spots. There were reasons for the

---

[2] Stanford University (http://orbis.stanford.edu) has developed an interactive map of the Empire which demonstrates the real-time-and-cost impacts of classical modes of transportation.

[3] Emperor Septimius Severus (193-211) managed to confuse the issue thoroughly for historians by stationing a new legion, *II Parthica*, about a day's march outside Rome, and everyone (in the twentieth century) assumed it was a 'strategic reserve'. It wasn't; its function was regime preservation, to counterbalance the Praetorian Guard in Rome, much as the elite Kantemir and Taman (Army) and Dzherzhinsky (KGB) Divisions balanced each other in bases around (not in) Moscow under the USSR—and still do. But Rome was two weeks' march from the nearest frontier.

organizational mutation, but they had less to do with grand strategy and more to do with regime preservation.[4]

As for 'preclusive defence', three hundred and fifty thousand men in thirty legions strung out from Carlisle to Beersheba were not going to 'preclude' anything. What the Romans were practicing was active deterrence. They were practicing it on a scale, over a time frame, and with a degree of success never before seen in history and rarely since, but they had neither the conceptual framework nor the vocabulary to describe what they were doing. They may have created practices that Western practitioners of military science, two thousand years later, have theorized—but they are hardly to blame for that![5]

When the deterrent collapsed, as it did in the third century, one response was to keep the Emperor near the frontiers. Another was to fortify absolutely everything

---

[4] Stationing *Parthica* at Albanum was an ad hoc measure of Severus'. It assumed that the Emperor would normally be in Rome. But beginning in his time, the Emperor and his guard units were increasingly to be found close to the frontiers, partly because they were needed there, and partly because an Emperor who had gained his Purple by revolution could never trust an expeditionary force away from his gaze—often enough not even directly under it.

[5] For that matter, no statesman before 1950 would have recognized the word 'deterrent' as it is now used in strategic theory. Ronald Syme (*The Roman Revolution*) has an unkind but trenchant aside on the tendency to drown modern military officers in operational theory and doctrine.

everywhere.[6] We have no way of knowing whether such a broad and uniform response—unsettlingly reminiscent of the American 'homeland security' reaction to events post-9/11—was evidentially justified. The Imperial government clearly thought it was.

And for more than five hundred years the Imperial Army evolved on the fly to meet threats, perceived and otherwise.

The Amateurs: The High Command

From start to finish, the Republic was run by noble amateurs. It took astonishingly long[7] after the legislated foundation of the Empire in 27 BCE for the government to begin professionalizing its public service even at the highest levels. Augustus took power with a coterie of very able men who had helped him win the Civil Wars. They were supplemented by members of his own family who were also, by and large, very capable. He outlived them all except Tiberius, who was possibly the most able of the lot. But the use of close supporters, family, and

---

[6] Roman installations of the early Empire (including Hadrian's Wall) were not meant for fighting. The border installations were anchor-points for controlled zones, meant to manage local movement, and, frankly, to impress the local residents. They succeeded; one stretch of the German *Limes* is known to this day as the Devil's Wall (*Teufelsmauer*).

[7] This depends on your perspective. In 1910 there was nothing like a large professionalized public service as we know it in either Canada or the United States.

freed slaves—an act that came as naturally to a Roman as breathing—delayed the creation of an institutional public service until the reign of Claudius (43-54 CE). For its first seventy-five years the Empire was improvising its entire machinery of government.[8]

But legions had to be commanded and provinces governed, and a system evolved slowly. Tiberius left his good governors in place for many years at a stretch (they weren't that easy to come by; Pontius Pilate was just one in a series of outstandingly terrible prefects of Judaea).

In the course of the first century, a system developed that saw governors of provinces, who might have up to four legions under them, appointed as *Legati augusti pro Praetore* ('Augustan Legates with the rank of Praetor'), and the legionary generals were given postings (two to five years) as *Legati legionis*. Appointed around the age

---

[8] An early sign that this might be a problem came along in 26 BCE when Augustus decided that he needed someone to run the City of Rome for him on a full-time basis. He appointed a distinguished Senator, P. Valerius Messalla Corvinus, to a sort of Mayorship with the revived Republican title of City Prefect (*Praefectus urbi*). Messalla lasted about two weeks before quitting, saying that he had no idea how to do his job. The position lapsed for another ten years.

The first Praetorian Prefect (*Praefectus praetorio*) was appointed only in 2 BCE. The office was made notorious by Sejanus of *I, Claudius* fame who made himself quasi-dictator when Tiberius retired from Rome. But the position—usually held by a pair of Prefects after Sejanus—did not assume regularized functions at least until Nero's reign (54–68).

of forty, they would have had no military experience except for their mandatory one year as Senatorial Tribune (one per legion) in their early twenties. Second-tier posts were held by the second order of nobility, the Equestrians, in origin as amateur as the Senators.

Western culture has evolved far away from amateurism in government, except for our political class of elected officials who are increasingly excluded by conflict-of-interest sensitivities from doing much that they actually have experience in. But it is well worth remembering that until the Cardwell Reforms of the 1870s, all officers' commissions in the British Army were purchased, and the British Empire in its prime was run by as enthusiastic (and eccentric) a bunch of noble amateurs as anything Rome ever laid claim to. In writing *The Decline and Fall of the Roman Empire* in the late 1770s, Edward Gibbon had nothing to say about professionalism in government; it was as alien to his age as to that of Augustus.[9]

---

[9] Similar circumstances beget similar remedies. With a seven-day communications lag between the Praetorium of the Army of Upper Germany at Mainz and the Palace at Rome, the capital had no choice but to leave the local commanders great freedom of action, which seems to have been delegated all the way down to the detached-duty centurions on the frontier. British commanders anywhere in the world perforce operated under similar loose rein. Both Empires occasionally paid a stiff price, but on the whole it worked. No ruler of either Empire ever watched an enemy leader being killed in real time, live from the Situation Room.

Generalship: The Home Study Way

There was never anything like a War College. But there were War Studies. As noted in Chapter One, Classical society had a very active and widespread publishing industry. Greeks and Romans both loved *how-to* books and lectures, and they published them for just about everything—warfare included.

The military-studies mania seems to have taken off in Greece right at the end of the Peloponnesian War around 404 BCE, when there was a surplus of unemployed officers around. By 400 BCE there were complaints about the glut of military studies professors in Athens. The Romans inherited the military home-study tradition.[10]

At least one Roman senior official had issues with the amateurist approach. Julius Frontinus, who had a brilliant public service career in the late first century, seems to have got his start in publishing by writing his own briefing notes for his various positions. The outstanding product of his that remains to us is the *Waterworks of Rome*, dating from his term as Commissioner of Aqueducts beginning in 95. In the form we have, it seems to have been an official report worked up from his due diligence, but he makes clear that a newly appointed senior official needs to *do* his due diligence.

Regrettably we have only one chapter of Frontinus on military affairs, but he tells us that his theme across

[10] See 'Teach Yourself How To Be a General' by Dr. Brian Campbell, *Journal of Roman Studies* (1987) for a review of the Greek and Roman military self-help publishing industry.

the board is: you will have a very skilled staff, but its members are *'merely the hands and instruments of the organizing intelligence'*. You, and only you, must get to know enough about your portfolio to take initiatives and make sensible decisions. For a general this would mean knowing the basics of manoeuvre and deployment, morale, psychological operations,[11] logistics, and getting to know your senior professionals really well. Frontinus' time as a Governor was spent in Britain in 74-78 while the frontier was still being pushed forward, security was questionable, and logistics and intelligence were vital.[12] He knew what he

---

[11] The surviving military handbooks, both Greek and Roman, lay heavy emphasis on stratagems (Frontinus' surviving piece is called *Stratagemata*). Soviet/Russian tradecraft calls them *maskirovka* and *provokatsiya*; deception and disruption. Campbell seems to have some issues with the concept that a list of stratagems could be all that useful—when read as a list they can look pretty jejune—but he may discount too much the actual difficulty of obtaining reliable field intelligence. Stratagems are, above all, psychological warfare, and after the Crimean episode of 2014, no one can say they aren't effective.

A typical example from Frontinus: *when the Emperor Domitian proposed to invade Dacia [Rumania], he gave it out in advance that he was headed north to take the census in Gaul, so that the Dacians did not put themselves in a state of defence.* That one is strongly reminiscent of Vladimir Putin's deception of attending the 2008 Olympic Games in Beijing while readying an attack on Georgia. (But Putin gets far too much credit for his stratagems.)

[12] His previous assignment had been on the Rhine, helping Petilius Cerialis suppress the Batavian Revolt of 70 CE, which we will visit in Chapter Five. Before that, he had been City Prefect during the exciting

was talking about; under-briefed officers might not survive Britain.

The other vital ingredient in the education of a senior commander was 'home schooling', that is, family tradition. Most modern nations have military families whose members have risen to command through several generations. In the Roman Republic, *every* leading family had that tradition, generation after generation. Moreover, until the end of the second century BCE, even aristocratic housing was very modest. Four generations would live together in conditions that astonished the generation of Cicero's day a century later. 'The ways of the elders' (*mos maiorum*) were fetishized, and the younger generation could hardly fail to learn in such an environment. There would have been endless stories and lessons told over dinner—the 'war story' has been denigrated as a teaching device only in our own day[13]—and if somebody didn't make it home from the wars one day, that was as good a

---

and dangerous Year of Three Emperors in 68-69. He was sixty when he took the waterworks job; a Roman public servant's life was nothing if not varied. He was followed in Britain by the equally capable Agricola.

[13] Sir Lawrence Freedman in *Strategy: A History* (2013), while dissecting a broad range of (mainly unsatisfactory) theories of business, political, and military strategy, notes that 'storytelling' did make a comeback in corporate strategic theory in the 1990s. It was not successful because the stories could not take into account all important variables and might be biased from the get-go. The method may be more useful in discussing clearly circumscribable military campaigns than long and complex corporate processes.

lesson as a Triumph, in addition to being a family shame that had to be avenged.

Lucius Aemilius Paullus,[14] who defeated Perseus of Macedonia in 168 BCE, told the story forever after about the 'shock and awe' (his words) that he felt when he saw the phalanx come rolling over the field of Pydna into his front line—and he must have been ridden by the shade of his father, Lucius Aemilius Paullus, who never made it home from the disaster at Cannae in 216.

As the Senatorial aristocracy was broadened and diffused during the first two centuries of the Empire, there was inevitable watering down of family tradition, but it was supplemented by the growth of structured career paths for Senators and Equestrians alike. By the end of the first century, a Senator could opt for, effectively, either a 'military stream' or a 'civil stream', and the Equestrian Order had similar options. Almost everyone in harness would know each other (which made the occasional civil wars even more unpleasant).

This all needed management. Political reliability was a key factor (and anyone who has ever served in even a democratic military will readily confess that 'politics' is the major determinant in the most senior appointments). The Palace had to manage about sixty Senatorial-level command appointments, with an average turnover of

---

[14] Paullus grew up with four generations under one roof. The personal booty he brought home from Macedonia was the first silver plate ever seen in the house. He seems to have been a fascinating and complex man, well-drawn by Plutarch.

perhaps 20% per year. One of the Palace ministries (Claudius established four between 41 and 54) was responsible for the appointments process; probably the Petitions Branch (*a libellis*).

The nasty and lengthy eastern and northern wars of Marcus Aurelius (160-180) seem to have accelerated career specialization. By the early 170s, probably every Senator who couldn't make the grade in a field command had been weeded out. We begin to see appointments from some 'non-mainstream' backgrounds, including the future Emperor Pertinax[15] and the slightly-better-connected African future Emperor Septimius Severus, both of whom won command through merit. By the time of the rebellion of 238 CE against Maximinus Thrax (Chapter Seven), the Senators currently resident in Rome constituted a professional talent pool sufficient to organize a successful ad hoc defence of Italy against a large and experienced army corps.

The Professionals: Prefects, Tribunes, and Centurions

The appointments that were counted on to keep the Army going were the career positions. All could be sourced from the provincial aristocracies, which gave them an incentivized buy-in to the Imperial power structure itself. Centurions could also be promoted from the ranks, though we can imagine that the more

---

[15] Who had started his working life as a grammar teacher and was allegedly the son of a freed slave.

prestigious post-Service appointments were probably had by the 'gentlemen' officers.

At the command level below the Senatorial Legate (*Legatus legionis*), an Imperial legion also possessed six Tribunes who—theoretically—outranked the centurions. The senior one—the 'Broad-striper'[16]—was a one-year entry-level Senatorial appointment and it was essentially a get-out-of-it-what-you-put-into-it assignment. It was all the military service a Senator might see before he got his legion ten years or so later.

There were also five 'Narrow-stripers' of the Equestrian Order and *they* were the next generation of military management. They came from regional aristocracy by recommendation of a Governor and had begun their careers as commander (Prefect) of a junior Auxiliary unit. They were fast-track professionals in what may have amounted to a field-grade command internship, and they were headed for senior centurion appointments or major Auxiliary commands elsewhere in the military structure. The tribunate gave senior management a chance to vet them under closer scrutiny than an independent command would allow.

Although every source we have lays immense stress on the need for exemplary logistics work, we have no indication of when in a man's career he might pick up the skills needed to do the job. One possibility might be that the Equestrian Tribunes spent a lot of their 'internship' learning staff work and logistics on the job, as this was

---

[16] *Tribunus laticlavus*; Senators wore a broad purple stripe on their tunics, the Equestrian Order a narrow one, so: *Tribunus angusticlavus*.

probably their only learning time together in a major base as not-quite line officers.

The top tier of the centurionate, the *Primi ordines*, was the institutionalized field command cadre of the Army. In modern terms, it's permissible to think of the *Primus pilus* ('First File') of a legion as about Brigadier equivalent and his four First Cohort colleagues as Colonels. They would be the men who, by and large, made and unmade Emperors in the bad days of the third century: the Gamal Nassers of their day.[17] Finally there was a professional Warrant Officer category (the top rank translates as 'Officer Candidate', *optio ad spem ordinis*). Many modern armies including the Soviet Army have not had professional non-commissioned officers.

As the legions settled down into more or less permanent residence in bases mainly along the frontier,[18] they tended by osmosis to acquire administrative and governance functions. The Auxiliary units in their vicinity tended to become associated with them, and, since there was no other qualified cadre, the centurions furnished the talent for general administration.[19] As the great legionary bases became the centres of military districts, administration

---

[17] They also apparently made a lot of money post-retirement or even pre-retirement. In the third century, there was apparently a special surtax on the income of retired First Centurions.

[18] This did not happen overnight. Entire legions still could be and were transferred up to the third century.

[19] The paper establishment of a legion was fifty-nine centurions. Off the battlefield, the unit simply did not need that many, so they were available for other responsibilities.

elaborated with them, and we see the emergence of centurions assigned to specific non-command duties. In Ankara at one point, two were needed for traffic control. Dr. M. C. Bishop notes that there is evidence from five inscriptions of 'regional centurions' around the Empire (at Vindolanda near Hadrian's Wall, Bath, Ribchester, Mihailovgrad in Bulgaria, and 'somewhere in Egypt'). All of these locales qualify as 'frontier areas', or at least ones requiring close supervision.[20]

The Organization

Republican Armies were an assembly of conscript units for particular campaigns. By the beginning of the first century BCE the recruiting base was slowly converting to a salaried long-service model, but by 27 BCE the heavy infantry citizen legion of ten cohorts and up to five thousand men was still very much a tactical formation, rather like a Napoleonic division of 1804-1815. Its design function was to fight (and do engineering as part of war-fighting), and it did nothing else other than foraging. 'Other arms' (except for

---

[20] The job description was probably not far from that of the tribal agent on the Northwest Frontier of India in Rudyard Kipling's time. Among other things, it would involve getting into full rig every once in a while and stomping with your half-century into a village full of guys ripped on rotgut mead and testosterone and brandishing sharp instruments, to supervise the tribal markets/elections. Civil-military relations and counter-insurgency don't change greatly over the millennia.

artillery which was organic to the legion) were provided by the Auxiliary service, mainly composed of non-citizens.

By the third century the Army had become a bureaucratic machine with a scope unrivalled until the nineteenth century. It had also become an institution unto itself with a corporate agenda that may or may not have paralleled the agenda of the upper classes and current Emperor, and by the end of the third century it had effectively become the State.[21]

How the Army was organized at any given point, and especially how it fought at tactical level, is a subject that has been fought over harder than some of the original battles.[22] The 'peacetime' structure—like all

---

[21] The early Imperial public service outside the Palace itself was at all times a military service, since the Republic had had no civil servants at all. By the early fourth century, most government officials never saw a sword, but they all wore the military belt (*cingulum*) and as late as the reign of Justinian were enrolled in a notional 'legion', *II Adiutrix*. Originally a real legion raised in 69-70 (*'adiutrix'* means 'reinforcement'), it served for centuries at Budapest (Aquincum). When the Army of the Danube became the core around which an 'army of national salvation' formed after the catastrophe of the mid-third century, it seems to have mutated into an administrative legalism. There are no attestations for it as a fighting unit after about 293.

[22] Contrary to Greek military handbooks, which deal very precisely with fieldcraft, Imperial-era texts give us no real idea what actually went on at small-unit level once the advance sounded. The phalanx was rigid by design; the legion was flexible, and commanders had to leave unit handling in combat to the line

armies, the Imperial Army spent most of its time at peace—shows a remarkable degree of elaboration and flexibility. On the one hand, officers were constantly rotating among units and operational theatres (Britain, the Rhine, the Danube, and Syria were the major ones) so that experience and practices tended to be shared. On the other hand, operational conditions in Britain had little in common with those in Mesopotamia, and in the space of ten years, officers and men might see both. As the operational environment became more complex, the tendency increased for detachments from

---

officers, who didn't need handbooks. A few attested formations (like the famous walking pillbox, the *testudo*) aside, all modern speculation on fieldcraft is exactly that. Since about 1970 some very skilled re-enactor groups collaborating with scholars have contributed hugely to our knowledge of how things might have worked.

The most famous military writer of all, Flavius Vegetius, wrote at the very end of antiquity. Dr. M. C. Bishop kindly points out that his work is a sort of ancient Wikipedia article into which a variety of older sources have been indiscriminately dumped—a metaphorical beaver dam across the stream of history. We think his description of the *antiqua legio* might owe a lot to Frontinus. But we'll never know. Therefore, using him to reconstruct legionary organization and fieldcraft at any given time is...'difficult'. Bishop and Coulston think it may be a good snapshot of the third century Severan legion.

Ironically, while Vegetius has driven generations of scholars to drink, the audience he was actually writing for—the policy-makers— had no problems applying his advice effectively when at last in the fifteenth century conditions were again right for the creation of large infantry armies. He has been 'in print' ever since he first wrote.

several units to be brigaded as what the twenty-first century calls a battlegroup (*vexillatio*: a 'banner') for service 'out of area'.

A team from the Ermine Street Guard re-enactor unit (UK) lays and loads a field ballista (aka 'scorpion') for a high-trajectory shot. This looks like a mid-first-century model; second-century models had rainproof skein cylinders (shown on Trajan's Column), and third-century models dropped the cylinders and went to an all-metal frame. (Ermine Street Guard)

The Technology

Classical technology, unlike modern technology, was never able to achieve the critical mass necessary to sustain itself and keep growing. In a particular time and place something would bootstrap, then get lost again only to re-emerge elsewhere and later.[23]

This can be irrationally infuriating to us moderns. The Romans *should* have had the heliograph or the steam engine. They were certainly capable of them, but they never developed them. One of the irritating minor questions is, with all that engineering talent, why didn't they have the wheelbarrow?[24] One simple answer may be that on the march, dozens of light wicker baskets for earth-hauling are far easier to carry than a far smaller number of wheelbarrows.

The big exception is artillery. As late as 1815 the Duke of Wellington's officers were acutely aware that the Romans had had field artillery that was superior to theirs in every way—and smokeless and nearly recoilless. The extent to which the Romans exploited this capacity (as usual, Hollywood notwithstanding) is still being understood, but the finds at the Harzhorn battlefield (Chapter Six) are demonstrating the power of their field artillery at the peak of its development.

The difference lies in research and development. Artillery was nonexistent until the beginning of the fourth century BCE, when the dictator Dionysius of Syracuse, who had the resources and the need, founded the world's

---

[23] 'Greek fire' was by no means a new invention, though it may have been the most effective formulation. Pliny the Elder understood the problem of technological critical mass, and bemoaned the lack of interest by the Imperial government in research and development.

[24] Perhaps they did and we just haven't found one. We do keep on finding amazing things, like the 'Roman Army Knife'...

first defence research institute. He invited scholars and artisans from around the known world and paid them top drachma. From a standing start they invented both arrow-throwing and stone-throwing catapults.

Moreover, the effort was not a one-off. Dionysius' institute operated for generations, and Archimedes of Syracuse (d. 212) was its ultimate product, the Wernher von Braun of his day, which is why the Romans wanted to capture him so badly.

The Empire had scarce resources and needed all the force multipliers it could get. Augustus had calculated to a nicety what size of an army the Empire needed and could support, and his calculations were remarkably accurate. But the financial strain was never-ending, and no legionary commander could ever have left on posting without a resounding reminder from the Praetorian Prefect ('*Now* look, *Legate...*') of what his men were worth and the penalty for throwing them away. Like Western armies of today, the Imperial Army was risk-averse to a fault, and like Western armies of today, it substituted technology for men wherever feasible. Artillery technology improved to the point where in around 90 CE, Frontinus could declare that it had reached a point beyond which no improvement was possible. Wellington's staff would not have disagreed.

Apocrypha I: 'Now *look*, Legate...'

The pre-posting briefing is a fixture in history. Every regime that could call itself organized has evolved some way of making sure that governors or generals heading out on assignment at least have their metaphorical shoelaces tied when they leave the capital.

Early on in the Empire, certainly by Nero's time, a great deal of responsibility for this briefing process would have fallen to the Praetorian Prefect. The Legates-designate would have shown up at the Palace to get briefed on perquisites, personnel in positions, and whatever was in the archives about their slice of frontier. They would collect their non-transferable postal warrants. In the case of one Petilius Cerialis, Legate-designate of the Ninth Legion in about 59 CE, he would be shown in to the farewell interview with the Praetorian Prefect, S. Afranius Burrus. Burrus had started life as an accountant. It stuck out a mile.

> *Young Cerialis. I thought we'd be seeing you about now. Sit yourself down, honourable sir.*
>
> *<checks notes> Senator the Honourable Quintus Petilius Cerialis Caesius Rufus, law Praetor two years ago, Quaestor of the Treasury eight years ago, Broad-stripe Tribune in XXII Primigenia ten years ago under Statilius Nasica, and you survived both him and his wife in one piece, which is an accomplishment of sorts...*
>
> *First cousin to Senator the Right Honourable Titus Flavius Vespasianus, ex-consul. An interesting tidbit for the resume, though you might mention to your cousin that his tendency to drift off at unfortunate moments is drawing attention.*

Commissioned by Nero Augustus Caesar etc. etc. as Legatus legionis, to command the Ninth Legion Hispana, at the camp of Lindum in the Province of Britain, under proconsular command of the Right Honourable Gaius Suetonius Paulinus. Codicils signed by Nero Augustus Caesar, dated the Kalends of April, and countersigned this day by...me.

Now look, Legate.

Have you any idea on earth what it costs the Emperor to recruit, train, feed, house, equip, pay, pension and bury every one of those eight-thousand-odd SOBs you're being sent out to command? Because I'm going to tell you now that it costs six hundred and seventy five sesterces per man per year and that doesn't count horses, horse feed, army mules, road work, payoffs to contractors and bribes to the tribes in the quiet sectors to be good little boys.

You think you're going out there to advance the glory and power of the Senate and People of Rome with a side-order of decorations for Q. P. Cerialis. Well you're not. You have an active province there, you might see some campaigning. But you're going out to keep your little bit of this Empire under wraps by whatever means is most effective, quietest and cheapest. The Emperor has exactly twenty-seven legions to do that job for him and I won't hide from you that the Palace is taking a long hard look at the British commitment. Paulinus is our best commander right now after Corbulo, he's our last throw of the dice in that rathole and he knows it. If you waste even one century of those men on some harebrained scheme for the greater glory of Rome, you'd better hope that the little blue Brits[25] kill you first because if they don't I'll see to it personally.

Sextius Julianus is your Primus Pilus, thirty-five years in the Service, sixteen of them in Britain. He went in with Vespasian and the Second in the original force in case you don't know that already. You listen to what he has to tell you, you keep the locals quiet, you do a half-decent job and if we're both lucky I'll see you again in two or three years. Good afternoon to you honourable sir, have a fine farewell dinner and a glorious posting, and don't forget to sign for your postal warrants, first desk on the left as you go out.

Hail Caesar.

---

[25] Romans were not very imaginative with their ethnic slurs. *Graeculi* ('Little Greeks') or *Britunculi* ('Little Brits')—the latter in an intelligence assessment, no less—seems to have been about the extent of it.

Chapter Three

Unfamiliar Territory:
Regime Change in the East

Tell me how this ends.

— *Gen David Petraeus, US Army, Iraq, March 2003*

We begin in the middle. On March 7, 161 CE, the Emperor Antoninus Pius passed away peacefully at his summer home at Lorium. The Emperor Marcus Aurelius assumed the Purple. It was a seamless transition, but on hearing the news King Vologaesis IV of Parthia, out east in the Land Between the Rivers, decided that the change in regime was a perfect moment for a change of regime, and promptly overthrew the King of Armenia, a Roman nominee.

Naturally this meant war.

The moment sums up the whole of political relations between Rome and her Eastern neighbour for about six hundred and fifty years, longer by half than the modern West as we define it has existed. The enduring question is, *why?*

The buzzwords of international relations evolve rapidly. 'Regime change' and 'nation building' have been in play only since around 2002. They have come to signify a misguided intervention in the affairs of another state, with the intention of, respectively, removing an objectionable regime, and installing a system of governance that the intervenor believes is more in accord with the wishes of the people concerned, or is at least more in accord with the values of the intervenor. Following American and Western experiences in Iraq and Afghanistan, they have also come to imply 'getting in over your head', in cultures so fundamentally alien that even if there is a coherent strategy going in, the experience may be nasty, brutish, long, unsatisfying, and (as seen in Libya in 2011 and Syria/Iraq in 2011-14) may have unforeseen consequences across the existing world order.

Trying to apply the 'nation-building' paradigm to the early Empire is pointless. In a very restricted sense the Romans were doing it everywhere they went that wasn't the Hellenized world, but it had very little in common with the modern proposition.[1] 'Regime change' is another story. The Romans kept the local elites, law codes, and currencies around while throwing out any rulers who would not play, but as they intended to stay for a few centuries themselves, any comparison with the modern interpretation is moot, with one great exception: the Parthian Empire.

Parthia stretched from Mesopotamia (now Iraq to eastern Syria) to around Afghanistan, essentially in the

---

[1] In later centuries, the Eastern Empire sent out missionaries to convert foreign nations to Christianity as a key element of an alliance 'package'. This might be viewed as limited-objective 'nation-building', but if so, it had as little success as the current variety. Thus Russia became Orthodox, and that worked out well for Constantinople. Bulgaria and Serbia less so; they now simply ravaged Roman lands under the sign of the Cross.

lands traversed by Alexander the Great and later ruled by the 'Successor' kings of the Seleucid dynasty. After Rome's victory over Carthage in 202 BCE, Parthia was the first nation that she encountered which could even pretend to be an equal power. For about three hundred years the Romans tried repeatedly and determinedly to effect 'regime change' in Parthia, every time without success and at huge cost in money, lives, and prestige. When the regime finally did change in the early third century, it was not the Romans who changed it, and it changed very much to their disadvantage.

Again: *Why?* What was the source of such an irreconcilable conflict? The answer lies somewhere between cultural and geopolitical, but may also have distressingly much to do with Sir Edmund Hillary's reason for climbing Mount Everest.[2] Animosities become self-perpetuating.

Rome became 'involved' in the Eastern Mediterranean on an escalating basis from the early second century BCE onward. We may or may not choose to believe contemporary Roman writers when they say that they kept getting dragged involuntarily into local disputes among the fractious Hellenic states, though there is something to that. Modern experience certainly provides analogies; US involvement in Vietnam from 1954 onward comes to mind. There was always a faction in both Senates that believed strongly that over-involvement was a bad idea. But Rome, like all great powers in any age, had a tendency to throw its weight around. In 168 BCE, with Rome heavily engaged against Macedonia, and

---

[2] Because, of course, it was there.

supported by no more force than his commission of noble advisors, the Senate's representative Popilius Laena drew the first recorded 'line in the sand' around King Antiochus IV of Syria and told him to make up his mind about invading Egypt before he stepped out of it. It worked because the King himself was inside it, three feet from the old man and his stick. It worked less well somewhat later for an American President; in these matters chutzpah is everything.

After about 146, when Corinth and Carthage were destroyed in spectacular acts of reprisal, any show of reluctance was dropped and Rome simply did as it pleased in the East. It became a happy hunting ground for Senators and carpetbaggers. Local kings and warlords regularly and naively tried to use the Romans as outside leverage against each other, usually finding out in the event that the Romans had walked off with the stakes.[3]

In 120 Mithridates VI became King of Pontus, a small kingdom on the south coast of the Black Sea. By the time he died in 63 after a stupefying long reign, he had gained, then lost, control over most of Anatolia (western and northern Turkey) and the Greek cities of the Anatolian seacoast, and he was allied with the Kingdom of Armenia, which at the time was centred on Lake Van in eastern Turkey, and included the headwaters of the Tigris and Euphrates (Osrhoene, now Kurdistan). He took forever to be defeated in three wars, by Sulla, Lucullus, and Pompey

---

[3] For sex, intrigue, and senseless violence, *Game of Thrones* can't even touch Eastern dynastic politics of the day.

in turn, not least because the Roman Republic was then engaged in its first spasms of political collapse.

The Debated Lands: Upper Mesopotamia, Osrhoene, and Greater Armenia (Kieran McAuliffe)

During the First Mithridatic War in 92, the later dictator Sulla was involved in a minor clash with the Armenians and in the course of it had an historic first contact on the Euphrates with the Parthians, whom he saluted as 'friends of the Roman people'.[4] It was about the last time they were even remotely friends for nearly seven hundred years.

The lands Mithridates conquered in Anatolia and toward Mesopotamia presented a conundrum to any ruler. The city states of the seacoast were Hellenized. The hinterland was not. Once beyond the coast and into the inner lands of the Anatolian plateau, or beyond the coastal mountains of the Levant into inner Syria, you returned to a land that the Persian Kings of Kings had ruled, that still worshipped local varieties of the Sun God (Baal), that spoke Syriac/Aramaic and other indigenous languages instead of Greek, and that farther east followed a very early form of Zoroastrianism.[5] Mithridates was a master propagandist. When it suited him, he stressed his Hellenic persona. When he had to appeal to other constituents, he stressed his affinity with Cyrus and Darius the Great. The Romans were comfortable enough with Hellenized city states; for one thing, they knew exactly where to grab them by the

---

[4] This was a usual first response to anyone Rome wanted to size up before taking on. See Ariovistus in Chapter Five.

[5] Zoroastrianism's early history under the first Persian Empire is vague. It was dualist in nature; acknowledging the power of Light (personified by Ahura Mazda/Ormazd) and the power of Darkness (personified by Ahriman). From it were syncretized many dualist beliefs down the ages, including that of the Manichees. There are still Zoroastrians in Iran and South Asia. But by the First Centuries BCE/CE, as David Potter puts it, in its original form it had dwindled to a set of Hellenized fairy tales.

power matrix. The more oriental cultures were far less comprehensible, and far less docile.[6]

Pompey finally defeated Mithridates in 63 BCE and set about imposing a 'settlement' on the Anatolian and Syrian lands. Sketched broadly, the settlement consisted of setting up direct Roman rule of the Hellenized coastwise lands from the Black Sea around to Syria, and a *cordon sanitaire* of client kingdoms farther east. The outer belt was scarcely Hellenized at all. The client kings were self-governing and ungarrisoned by Roman troops but had to clear their foreign policy with Rome. It was a sensible strategy for a regime that did not want to get pulled in out of its depth.[7]

Beyond them lay Parthia in the lands of Mesopotamia (Iraq); farther east still, the 'lands of the Medes and the Persians' (Iran). The Parthians were a semi-nomadic people who had migrated westward from the Iranian plateau, expanding into the power vacuum left by the last Seleucid heirs of Alexander. They had not been in Mesopotamia for very long and in fact were still looking for a westward frontier when they encountered Sulla at the Euphrates.

---

[6] Mithridates means 'gift of Mithras', who was a sub-deity in the Zoroastrian pantheon. In an ironic twist of fate, his worship became a mainstay of the Roman Army until the very end of paganism in the late fourth century (his birthday, by no coincidence, was December 25). Oriental culture as a whole was impenetrable to the Romans, but as with 'fusion' cultures today, specific elements could be borrowed and transplanted, often wildly out of context.

[7] Once he got past the 'Teenage Butcher' (*adulescens carnifex*) phase of his career, Pompey's settlements were usually very sensible.

The Parthian kingdom had its capital at Seleucia, not far from modern Baghdad, and what was important about Seleucia is that it was a 'fusion' city, populated by Greeks, Syrians, and Jews, and fully Hellenic in spirit. As long as the Parthian kings ruled from there, there was some kind of cultural bridge. They themselves were not very Hellenized and for most of the period spoke Pahlavi, an older form of Farsi. (No Parthian literature has descended to us.) They were a semi-feudal society, with seven great landowning families occupying the leading positions in the state. Compared to Rome's, their political structure was decentralized and weak.

Their strength, as Rome was about to find out, was in cavalry. They might field seven thousand fully-armoured heavy cavalry (*cataphracti*)[8] who could be more or less effective depending on circumstances, and up to forty thousand trained horse archers with the deadly recurve composite bow, who were fearsomely effective in any open country.

The strategic pivot was southern Armenia, insofar as whoever ruled Armenia controlled the headwaters of the Tigris and Euphrates, the only feasible route from Mesopotamia to the Mediterranean. The strategic constraints were then as they are now; the Syrian Desert is effectively impassible for armies, mechanized or otherwise.

---

[8] Known in the trade as *clibanarii*, 'boiler boys'. *You* try wearing a full set of iron scale armour in Iraqi temperatures. Canadian 'light infantry' who served in Kandahar will understand. With gratitude to Peter Brown for a delightful translation of the term.

Any borders drawn there were neither more nor less arbitrary and mutable than those established by the Sykes–Picot Agreement of 1916. The Syrian Desert and upper Mesopotamia were dotted by a group of oases and trading fortress-cities: Edessa (Urfa), Nisibis (Nusaybin), Amida (Diyarbekir), Hatra (al-Hadr), and farther west, Palmyra (Tadmor) which became famous and infamous to the Romans and Byzantines as they played saviours and spoilers, changed hands or failed to change hands over and over down the centuries.

In short, Rome's Eastern frontier was always going to be ill-defined and contentious wherever established, as long as there was someone to contend with. Parthia filled the prescription with Armenia as the strategic and political pivot, but Pompey had left Armenia basically friendly. That condition was susceptible to change without notice. Strategically, upper Mesopotamia is frighteningly close to Antioch, the capital of Syria, and to the Mediterranean (about 360 km between Antioch and Edessa). That was a strategic constant and a vulnerable re-entrant, but only a strategic threat if Parthia was actively hostile.

There were minor brushes until 54 BCE when the *triumvir* Marcus Licinius Crassus (of *Spartacus* fame) decided that his partners Pompey and Caesar were having all of the military glory while all he had was a lot of boring money. Anthony Blond in *A Scandalous History of the Roman Emperors* comments that his actions seem incomprehensible to us, as nobody expects a modern Wall Street plutocrat to go out and seek fame by personally invading somebody.[9] But the Roman system of government-by-amateur practically guaranteed that somebody would try this periodically, and in fact periodically several people did, often disastrously. Crassus merely achieved a more spectacular disaster than most.

Crassus got himself a proconsular appointment out East, raised eight legions,[10] borrowed some medium cavalry from Caesar in Gaul, and off he went.

A few months later he and most of his army were dead outside the town of Carrhae (Harran) in northern Mesopotamia, having stumbled across a desert in pursuit of an army that would not stand and fight and could shred even the *testudo* with sustained long-range arrow fire. Ten thousand made it back to Antioch, ten thousand

---

[9] It does give a new (old?) meaning to the phrase 'hostile takeover'.

[10] Crassus was the man who said that you couldn't call yourself rich unless you could outfit and maintain a legion for a year. Nowadays, he could at least do the outfitting by Web order from India; perhaps not quite 'period' and probably better made (which would not have bothered Crassus) but certainly more expensive (which would have). Re-enactors are constantly surprised to find that Roman production standards were 'ISO Good Enough to Win'. The Russian munitions industry follows the same standards template.

If you wish to try outfitting a legion at home (local public order and counter-insurgency by-laws may apply), remember that you also have to feed them, as Cicero found out one day when Caesar showed up for lunch with his bodyguard of two thousand men. Even in antiquity, two thousand box lunches didn't come cheap.

went into Parthian captivity, and some may or may not have wound up in Chinese service. Eight Eagles went with them. Crassus' head was sent to the Parthian King Orodes for a one-off appearance as a stage prop.

It was an unprovoked aggression and it essentially set the pattern for future Roman-Parthian relations— generational hostility, settling into an instructive pattern of peaking into warfare at intervals generally long enough that the decision-makers in Rome could forget what a disaster the last time had been. For the next fifty years Crassus' Eagles were the rallying cry in Roman propaganda. Ten years later Julius Caesar was outfitting an army in Macedonia for a revenge expedition when he was assassinated.

During the civil wars between Antony and Octavian, there was desultory warfare with Parthian forces (including a high-profile Roman defector, Quintus Labienus) but both sides had their own preoccupations. Rome spent twenty-five more years anticipating that Augustus would avenge Crassus once and for all, but he surprised public opinion by bringing off a negotiated return of the captive Eagles, and even some of the (by now very aged) prisoners in 2 BCE.

Half a century later hostilities again broke out over Armenia, where the Parthians had unexpectedly enthroned their own nominee as King. Nero's government sent out a 'star' general, Domitius Corbulo, who made the first iteration of a recurring discovery: that Roman troops in the Eastern bases became slack and demoralized, probably due to their being quartered in or too close to the cities where many of them had been recruited. After some prolonged and inconclusive fighting and a couple of swaps of Armenian candidates, Nero[11] and Corbulo negotiated a settlement with the Parthians whereby Parthia's nominee Tigranes would be King of Armenia but would receive his crown from Nero at Rome. The resulting coronation party was epochal, going down in history as 'the Golden Day', and for fifty years afterward, there was apparently a long, desultory, and dyspeptic 'Who lost Armenia?' debate at dinner parties in Roman power circles.

This may or may not have been one of the deciding factors in Trajan's campaign into Parthia in 114-117 CE. It makes little sense on the face of it, and may have been sheer vainglory; Trajan had been in the Purple since 98, was getting old, had had a solid (and strategically justified) victory in Dacia north of the Danube in 106, loved soldiering, and may simply have been looking for another victory at the end of his life. This time, for the first time in the Imperial period, the Romans were out for regime change, or more bluntly, conquest. They do not seem to have had much of an exit strategy beyond making northern Mesopotamia above Ctesiphon into a series of provinces.[12]

---

[11] Blond notes that at one point Nero suggested contributing to a peaceful settlement by getting up in front of the opposing army and crying. Wiser heads apparently persuaded him that this was not really an effective tool of conflict resolution.

[12] 'Trajan's Parthian War and the fourth century perspective' by C. J. Lightfoot in *Journal of Roman Studies* (1990).

Trajan ca 116: 'Arabia acquired' Collection of Mr. Roger Lucy

At least the Army seems to have been in better shape this time. Trajan concentrated about half the effective strength in the Empire into the expeditionary force; he may not have gone in with many fewer ground troops than US Gen Tommy Franks did from the southern end in 2003.[13] But he stripped effectives from the Danube, and as a result there seem to have been covering redeployments all along the other frontiers from Britain (Chapter Four) east to the Upper Danube.

Trajan first secured Armenia in 114 and put a Roman nominee on the throne. In 115 he campaigned in upper Mesopotamia (Kurdistan) with mixed success, then in 116 took Ctesiphon and was able to watch a ship set sail from Basra for India, regretting that he was too old to follow in the footsteps of Alexander.

---

[13] The campaigns into Parthia in the second through fourth centuries saw the biggest expeditionary forces and heaviest logistics the Empire ever mounted. Arther Ferrill in *The Fall of the Roman Empire: the Military Explanation* (1975) cites Ammianus' tale of a pile of cavalry fodder so huge that its collapse killed fifty men. Ammianus may have witnessed it.

We have no way of knowing how big a force Maximinus Thrax led into Germany in 235 (Chapter Six). It was not small, but not likely to have been as massive as any in the Eastern campaigns. In Germany, they were living off the country.

In 117 the operation blew up in his face, revealing to the Romans a secret of Empire that has become familiar to more modern campaigners including Napoleon and Hitler in Russia, and Brezhnev, Gorbachev, George W. Bush, and Obama in Iraq and Afghanistan, and, quite possibly, Putin in Ukraine: it is easier to take a country than to hold it. The Romans may legitimately have forgotten this because so much of their military experience after Carthage was with city-states or small autocracies, where it was actually possible to fix, hold, and destroy an enemy. But still, they might have remembered Spain and Britain and Greater Germany where things went less easily. Apparently 'lessons learned' were no more transmissible then than they are now.[14]

By 117 there had been no decisive battle. In a diffuse polity the loss of Ctesiphon meant very little. The Parthian army had retreated eastward but was intact. The strategic cities in upper Mesopotamia revolted and chased out the Roman garrisons. Meanwhile the expeditionary force got hung up on the siege of Hatra (al-Hadr in Iraq due west of Kirkuk) which was especially hard to take because the barren terrain made logistics difficult.

And then the Jews rebelled.

The Jewish revolt of 117 throughout the Eastern Roman Empire makes the modern *intifada* pale by comparison. The Jews had lost Jerusalem in 70 CE after a four-year revolt fought with unspeakable viciousness on both sides. Resentments had had nearly fifty years to fester, and when it became clear that Trajan was well

---

[14] And 'never fight a land war in Asia' no less relevant.

tied down in Parthia, revolts broke out in Cyrenaica (eastern Libya), Cyprus, Egypt, and Judaea itself. It is also said that the Jews were the prime movers of the risings in the newly occupied strongpoints in Mesopotamia.

The revolt directly threatened Roman supply lines. The siege of Hatra was not resolving well. Trajan crowned a puppet in Ctesiphon, declared victory, and pulled his whole force out to regroup on Antioch; he himself died en route. Hadrian became Emperor and promptly renounced all claims to the Parthian territories except for Armenia.[15] Nisibis became a great Roman fortress and lynchpin of the frontier, and the Romans of the fourth century tended to look back on Trajan as the Emperor who threw away a great victory when it was in his grasp.[16]

Although unsuccessful, the campaign is viewed by many scholars as the beginning of the 'eastward shift' of the Roman Empire which facilitated the cultural metamorphosis that in the end gave rise to late Roman and early Byzantine culture.[17] In the shorter term the extension of the frontier into Mesopotamia marked a

---

[15] He had to kill four of Trajan's field marshals to do it. It was a bad first step in relations with the Senate.

[16] They overlooked the fact that his victory hadn't lasted three years. Similar views have been expressed in our time about George H. W. Bush's decision to stop short of Baghdad.

[17] Peter Brown's *The World of Late Antiquity* (1971) pioneered this point of view. Only since then have researchers really examined the political influence of the interplay of cultures and faiths of the Roman eastern frontier.

shift in strategic balance whose results were not finally felt for another century.

Forty years passed and Marcus Aurelius became Emperor. The Parthians took advantage, as we have seen. (The ensuing disaster of 161 in Armenia may have been the one in which the Ninth Legion finally perished.) Marcus' field marshal Avidius Cassius again took Ctesiphon in 165, but plague—which might have been either smallpox or the true bubonic plague *Yersinia pestis*—broke out at the sack and proceeded to ravage the Empire. It remained sporadically endemic for close to a century and undoubtedly contributed to Rome's debility in the third century.

Septimius Severus ca 199: 'Arabia and Adiabene'. Collection of Mr. Roger Lucy

Again, Cassius does not seem to have been able to fix and engage the Parthian main force. The war ended with another Roman pullback. It seems likely that Parthia too was hard hit by the plague. If so, Rome was lucky because in 166 there began a series of high-intensity wars in the Upper Danube theatre against the south German peoples (Chapter Five) which strained the Empire's resources severely.

Thirty years later, in 195, Septimius Severus again attacked Parthia. He had just emerged from a civil war against a rival, Pescennius Niger, who had been based in Syria, and he may have felt that he needed to win the loyalty of Niger's legions. He was also married to a Syrian princess, Julia Domna of Emesa; these connections continued to deflect his dynasty's attention away from more traditional (and western) focal points for thirty-five years.

The war aims this time were somewhat different; Severus was out to annex the Syriac kingdom of Osrhoene (modern Kurdistan) in the upper reaches of the Tigris and Euphrates. He sacked Ctesiphon (again) and got hung up on the siege of Hatra (again). In fact he besieged the place twice, both times unsuccessfully.[18] The perennial problem of weak Eastern troops seems to have shown itself alongside inter-service jealousies. A particularly disastrous attack took place when the European legions (who had apparently been pulled back when they thought they could have taken the city) refused to support the Syrian formations (who were massacred as a result). Severus is said to have been in a foul mood (who can blame him?) at the ensuing council of war. Someone offered brightly that if Severus would give him 550 of the European troops,[19] he would take the city the next day. Severus shot back, 'And where would I get so many [loyal ones]?'[20]

Severus ended up establishing and garrisoning two provinces, Osrhoene and Mesopotamia. Both were well outside the Romans' sphere of cultural comfort, and

---

[18] Archaeological remains suggest that the town may have surrendered after the second siege.

[19] Effectively, a reinforced infantry cohort.

[20] Dio tells the story in his Book 76.

worse, represented a strategic over-extension. In Book 75.3.2 Dio Cassius offers one of those rare comments that illustrates that, whatever the deficiencies of a classical education may have been, a contemporary writer was no less capable of incisive criticism (*'Was it worth it?'*) than any modern pundit.

> He [Severus] used to declare that he had added a vast territory to the empire and had made it a bulwark of Syria. On the contrary, it is shown by the facts themselves that this conquest has been a source of constant wars and great expense to us. For it yields very little and uses up vast sums; and now that we have reached out to peoples who are neighbour of the Medes and the Parthians rather than of ourselves, we are always, one might say, fighting the battles of those peoples.

Dio, who had had some practical experience, grasped what the Beltway too often fails to: you may have all the client states you like, but the odds are that they will end up wagging the Imperial dog, usually at the most inconvenient time. If someone had offered Dio the term 'quagmire', he might well have taken it. (He didn't think highly of the British commitment either.)

The war of 195-202 was almost the last gasp of the Roman–Parthian struggle. Severus' son Caracalla tried to mount an offensive in 217, but he was assassinated that year and it petered out after an inconclusive battle in front of Nisibis shortly after. It was the last battle Romans and Parthians ever fought—but far from the last in that theatre.

It is hard to say whether the repeated large-scale wars with Rome fatally undermined the Parthian regime. It was never that coherent politically and was given to dynastic feuds. But in the early 220s a very strong contender for power emerged in a native Iranian dynasty, the Sassanians from around Fars, whose king Ardashir I destroyed the last Parthian king, Artabanus V, in 224 and crowned himself King of Kings in Ctesiphon.

Sea-change in the East: Shapur I, ca 240-270, King of Kings of Persia. Collection of Mr. Roger Lucy

The new regime was young, vigorous, and pushed a highly nationalist Iranian line including a revived, crusading Zoroastrianism.[21] Ardashir announced his claim to all the territories of the Persian Empire of Darius the Great (late sixth century BCE). Effectively that was all of the Roman Empire in the East, and Ardashir immediately began acting like he meant it. Alexander Severus, the last Severan, was forced to campaign against him less than successfully in 231-233. In 233, as we will see in Chapter Six, the Germanic federation of the Alemanni erupted across the Upper Rhine frontier and Rome's strategic centre of gravity shifted abruptly westward—for a little while.

---

[21] *The Roman Empire at Bay* by David Potter (2004, 2014) gives a thorough overview of the sea-change and its strategic implications.

The regime change in Parthia, which was certainly not anything that the Romans themselves perpetrated, had serious long-term consequences for them. Traditionally Parthia had been a very expensive punching bag for the Empire. The struggle now became ideological. Persia was an active threat and a resource sinkhole for the next three hundred years. Strategically, Hatra joined Nisibis as bulwarks for the Roman frontier. Armenia became a permanent Roman ally instead of a bone of contention. But at a time when she could least afford it, Rome became open to the permanent menace of simultaneous war in two theatres, European and Eastern. By 260 a Roman Emperor was prisoner in Persia.

Chapter Four

Modern Legend:
The Late, Great Ninth Legion

Sometime about the year 117 AD, the Ninth Legion, which was stationed at Eburacum where York now stands, marched north to deal with a rising among the Caledonian tribes, and was never heard of again.

During the excavations at Silchester nearly eighteen hundred years later, there was dug up under the green fields which now cover the pavements of Calleva Atrebatum, a wingless Roman Eagle, a cast of which can be seen to this day in Reading Museum. Different people have had different ideas as to how it came to be there, but no one knows, just as no one knows what happened to the Ninth Legion after it marched into the Northern mists.

—Rosemary Sutcliff

Thus, the Foreword to Rosemary Sutcliff's great young adult novel *The Eagle of the Ninth*, published in 1954 and often perhaps the only time that several generations of high school students ever met a Roman in literature.

In her way and her niche Sutcliff has done for Roman Britain something of what Shakespeare did for Caesarian Rome—if English is your first language and you're a non-specialist, chances are good that any impression you have of Roman Britain came from Sutcliff or Rudyard Kipling or both.[1] *Puck of Pook's Hill*, which inspired Sutcliff, is less read now than it once was, but if you've read it, then your impression of Hadrian's Wall[2] at the ending of its days is probably what Kipling (and Parnesius) gave you:

> *Just when you think you are at the world's end, you see a smoke from East to West as far as the eye can turn, and then, under it, also as far as the eye can stretch, houses and temples, shops and theatres, barracks and granaries, trickling along like dice behind—always behind—one*

---

[1] If you go on to look more deeply into Roman Britain, the strong impressions Sutcliff leaves can trip you up. I spent many years under the illusion that the breakaway Emperor Carausius had invented the camouflaged interceptor galleys of the *classis Britannica*. I would swear that I read this before I read *The Silver Branch*, in which she mentions 'a sad-eyed individual in the sea-green tunic of the scouting galleys'.

In fact, a third-century source (Philostratus, *Imagines*) says that Mediterranean pirates used blue-grey camouflage, and Vegetius claims that Julius Caesar introduced blue-green camouflage into British waters. Carausius logically then would have had them, but it's not documented. We can be sure he didn't invent them. (Neither did Caesar.)

[2] We are now pretty sure that the Romans actually called it Hadrian's Wall (*Vallum Aelii*) thanks to a nice piece of 'regimental silver' found in 2003. The reason we are only 'pretty sure' is because, as the British Museum notes, part of the inscription is 'very significant but more difficult to interpret'. That's the way it goes in Roman history.

*long, low, rising and falling, and hiding and showing
line of towers. And that is the Wall!*

And Sutcliff (and Marcus Aquila) probably gave you
your impression of the Wall at its birth sometime in the
mid-130s:

> *From Luguvallium in the west to Segedunum in the
> East the Wall ran, leaping along with the jagged
> contours of the land, a great gash of stonework, still raw
> with newness.*[3]

In 2011 two feature movies were made about *Legio IX
Hispana* and its fate. Cinematically it's doing better than
just about any modern unit except the Light Brigade. *The
Eagle* is a fine retelling of Sutcliff's original, and *Centurion*
a very passable survival tale in the manner of *Band of
Brothers*. Both do justice to Sutcliff's Wall as her hero
would have seen it.

---

[3] Sutcliff may have described more truly than she knew. Dr.
Bishop has kindly pointed out to me that recent air surveys suggest
fairly substantial pre-Wall settlement and long-standing field
boundaries in at least some sectors, and decreased crop production
north of the Wall after construction. Which means that, if it wasn't
quite the assorted very nasty Demilitarized Zones of the present day,
it was still probably not a fun place to spend time unless you were
somehow connected to the garrison. Living too close on the north side
was discouraged. The Regional Centurions would have refereed tribal
elections, supervised markets, and enforced restricted-zone access.

What was the Ninth Legion, what really happened to it, and where did the legend come from? The history and the mystery are one question, and the origin of the legend is quite another. Was word really passed down in some isolated glen over generations about how some remote ancestors of the Clan MacCreekie had wiped out a band of the hated Red Crests, *'and, Johnnie, 'tis said that the blood of the Red Crests runs in our line still'* …?

The Ninth Legion, titled *Hispana,* was one of the Original Twenty-Eight of the Imperial Army that Octavian 'Augustus' Caesar cobbled together from the bits and pieces of over sixty legions from his and Mark Antony's armies after the Battle of Actium in 31 BCE ended the Civil Wars. It had fought in Spain and did so again after 31, hence the surname. The Original Twenty-Eight became the Original Twenty-Five when Hermann the German had finished with P. Quinctilius Varus (and Rome's cross-Rhine ambitions) in 9 CE, and there were no additions for another twenty-five years or so, but by and large an amazing number of the units that began their careers with Augustus were still in active service four and even five centuries later. That beats any formation anywhere in the world today, though the Coldstream Guards (established in 1650) are getting close.

Though we know a lot about Rome and its Army, we know far too little that can be called a coherent narrative. We have nothing that even resembles a regimental history for the Ninth or any other legion, and for the whole four centuries or so only a few recorded anecdotes about individual units, like *XII Fulminata* ('the Thundering Legion') which became a Christian legend by the outright pilfering of a good pagan war story and propaganda meme from Marcus Aurelius' time (you can see it on his Column in Rome), but the name *Fulminata* came a long way first, the legends after. The rest is all archaeology and educated attempts to connect some very faded dots.

The Republican legions always had numbers; they never had names. They weren't permanent units; they were raised and disbanded annually. There were always Legions I through IV, the 'statutory' conscript legions. All others were supernumerary, probably numbered and renumbered each year at New Year's, and commanded by Senatorial Tribunes and Legates nominated by the consuls. During the war with Hannibal in the late third century BCE, the armies became massive and we see legionary series reaching into the twenties but still no names.

Afterward, as Rome acquired more and more standing overseas commitments, the principle of annual re-enlistment remained, but we can probably forgive ourselves for thinking that in an expeditionary force, the units that marched onto the field to be disbanded at New Year's looked remarkably like the new units that re-formed and re-took the oath a few minutes later, perhaps with some different senior officers.

Gaius Marius, the 'ploughboy from Arpinum', professionalized the Army at the beginning of the last century BCE. At that point any annual re-formation definitely became nominal (except perhaps for the four consular legions). He gave the legions their Eagles as the definitive unit standard and tutelary deity. After that, Roman warlords—which is what they were by then—

could have standing armies with a chance of developing unit identities and traditions.

As far as we know, the custom of giving titles to legions started around Julius Caesar's time. In Gaul in the 50s BCE he had his famous Tenth, which he called *Equestris*, which could mean either 'mounted' or 'knightly'. He had his Fifth, formed from non-citizen Gauls, called *Alaudae*, the Larks, which was the Gaulish national bird.[4] The name-giving took off during the Civil Wars, as you might expect in conditions where generals would do anything to keep up morale.

In 59 BCE Caesar invaded Gaul, and a Ninth Legion—apparently originally borrowed from Pompey—was with him. It was paid off at the end of the war against Pompey in 45 BCE, and when Octavian raised his armies after 44 for the wars against the Liberators and Antony, we don't know whether he reformed his Ninth on Caesar's veteran cadre or not, so continuity is questionable. However that may be, by the foundation of the Empire in 27 BCE, there was a Ninth Legion, it had been with Octavian for many years, it was called *Hispana* for its service in Spain, and it joined the Imperial order of battle.[5]

It stayed in Spain until about 19 BCE and then was transferred to Germany to fight in the German expansion campaigns to the Elbe under Drusus and Tiberius. It has

---

[4] Yes, Canadian Football League fans everywhere, Sen. Jules César owned a team called the Alouettes.

[5] The description of legionary nomenclature here is based firmly on Lawrence Keppie, *The Making of the Roman Army: From Republic to Empire*, 1998.

to have been involved in the Great Pannonian Revolt of 6-9 CE (almost every unit was at one time or another), and after that it was based in Pannonia, which is now Hungary and the former Yugoslavia.

In 43 it was assigned to Aulus Plautius' British expeditionary force along with three legions from the Rhine. It seem to have held the right flank of the advance into Britain, pushing north toward Lincoln while the Second went westward toward Devon and the Twentieth and Fourteenth went up the middle toward the Welsh border. That first phase went on for about eighteen years of sporadic heavy fighting. The Ninth found itself in the Lincoln area, possibly scattered in detachments rather than concentrated in base, and this is where the real story begins.

Rosemary Sutcliff calls the Ninth a cursed legion, and lays the curse squarely at Queen Boudicca's feet. Boudicca was the daughter of Prasutagus, King of the Iceni in East Anglia, a Roman client king. In about 60-61 he died and left the kingdom jointly to his daughters and the Emperor. This was common enough practice at the time; the Emperor got the land, the government got manpower and taxes, the royal family got a settlement, a tax write-off, and a bucket of medals, and everybody was happy. That didn't happen this time, perhaps partly because the legacy was not in the male line, but there were other forces in play.

The Governor Suetonius Paulinus was away from the centre of action with two legions in Anglesey attempting to wipe out the Druids' altars of mass destruction.[6] The financial Procurator Catus Decianus is described by Tacitus as rapacious, but he must also have been under heavy pressure from the philosopher Seneca and his friends in Rome where a market panic was in full swing. As befit their philosophy of charity and poverty, Seneca's crowd had huge loans out to the Iceni at monumental interest. Apparently Prasutagus had discovered the uses and abuses of credit on a grand scale. Boudicca probably found out the hard way when Seneca and company foreclosed.[7] They were Senators, Decianus was Equestrian Order; he wasn't going to put up a fight.

The Sutcliff version fingers the Ninth as enforcers for the collection of Prasutagus' debts. There is no recorded basis in history for this, but they were certainly in the right place at the right time. At any rate, Boudicca was flogged and her daughters raped, and then, says Sutcliff, she called down a curse on the whole legion and raised a revolt of astonishing ferocity.

If she really did it, it must have been one amazing curse because the Legate of the Ninth, Petilius Cerialis, who was apparently a known hothead, got wind of the rising and

---

[6] This was one of the pretexts for invasion about twenty years before. They actually found more concrete evidence than George W. Bush did in Iraq, though the range and destructive capacity were probably overrated.

[7] There is a theory that Nero's government was conducting a serious cost-benefit analysis of the British involvement at the time, which may have led to the panic. Contemporary writers did question ROI in Britain.

came pelting south with two thousand infantry and all of the cavalry. He got out of the ensuing massacre with most of the cavalry. Presumably he got out with the Eagle as well, or else it was safely back at headquarters. Maybe losing it to rebels didn't count and the government took a Murphy on that one after they'd won.[8] But most likely it wasn't with the detachment.

That was the first of the Ninth's British disasters. From then on, says Sutcliff, it had the reputation of a bad-luck legion, and a cursed one on top of that, and the unit began to rot from within.

Things like that do happen in the best of armies. We've seen examples of that closer to home in our own time—the Second Canadian Airborne's experience in Somalia comes to mind—and if you're another Legate somewhere in Germany and you have to send over a few hundred trained replacements that you know you're not going to get back, you are not likely to send the cream of the crop.[9] But eighty years of that kind of deterioration is a stretch. Simple geography tells us the Ninth were usually on the sharp end of the offensive in Britain in those years (Britain was all sharp end at the time). Someone in the higher command would have started noticing serious problems long before 117. But it's a great story.

---

[8] Decisions like these are always highly political. Quite a number of years later, the Canadian government made an entire battle in the Balkans disappear.

[9] Canadian military historian David Bercuson gives a very full account of the Airborne affair in *Significant Incident*. One of the problems was that they were dependent on other units for personnel.

In any case the Ninth moved up to York in about 71 as the frontier advanced, and then came Julius Agricola who decided to crown a very successful career by annexing all of Britain if he could. He was what we'd call a British country specialist in the Service, and the Emperor Domitian (who got along with his command staff if with nobody else) gave him an exceptionally long posting—78 to 85. He launched successive campaigns that took him as far as Clyde and Forth and into the Highlands.

He advanced in two columns, west and central, with the Ninth out of York forming the core of the central column, and the fleet covering the east coast. In around 82, somewhere around the Clyde, the Ninth got into trouble again. Tacitus says it was the weakest of the three legions, possibly owing in part to a battlegroup detached to Germany where Domitian was engaged with the tribes on the Rhine. It came under heavy night attack and Tacitus says that Agricola was forced to relieve it in a hurry.

From then to the celebrated 'disappearance' around 117-120, we know little of the unit's history. We have tile and brick stamps from Scalesceugh in the northwest, about 6 miles from Carlisle. The same from York, where the Legion was headquartered, most probably from the 85-105 era. There seems to have been a battlegroup from the Ninth on the Lower Rhine throughout that period, which makes sense as sea transportation from York to the Rhine mouth is easier than marching troops from the other two legions in the West of Britain for transhipment. What is interesting about tile stamps from both

Scalesceugh and the Lower Rhine is that they are numbered in what we are taught to think of as the classic Roman numeral nine—VIIII—while the headquarters stamps from York have what we are told is the mediaeval IX. Apparently both forms were in use in the first century in the Legion itself.

The last direct attestation we have for the Ninth anywhere is a major gate dedication at York dated to 108, just after Trajan's Second Dacian War. It would have been an obvious time to have a detachment on the Rhine, covering off for troop movements farther east. But things got much more difficult in 114.

In 114, as told in Chapter Three, Trajan invaded Parthia (Iraq) with apparently about the same number of ground troops as his American spiritual descendent did in 2003, and with similar results. By the time he died in 117, Rome was thoroughly bogged down.

There is every reason to think that the Western garrisons including Britain were heavily depleted for the Eastern commitment, though again the information is scrappy and archaeological. But over half the Army was engaged in the East, so there doesn't seem much alternative.

Word gets around to interested parties, and you don't need modern social media to get it around fast. If there really was a revolt in North Britain around 117, that would be the right time for it to happen and it would only be one of a number of such chain reactions in world history before modern communications. *Rome's in trouble in the East. Now's the time, boys.*

We *think* there was such a revolt. Two sources seem to refer to it, and one is by Marcus Aurelius' tutor Fronto, so within living memory. But dating is inexact. What we do know is that by 122, Hadrian was building his Wall—and we can't ignore the budgetary commitment involved in that sort of construction, not under Roman fiscal constraints—*VI Victrix* had moved to York from its previous posting in Spain, and the Ninth wasn't in Britain any more.

But was it destroyed by then? There is reason to think it wasn't. Inscriptions exist securely datable to the 140s and 150s, attesting to their subjects' service as junior officers in the Ninth at a time which would arguably have been in the mid-120s or later. But since you could be made Governor at any time within a ten- or fifteen-year span in your career, it doesn't necessarily seal it.

It was certainly off the order of battle by 165, because we have an order of battle from around that year and it's not listed. So we have a couple of possibilities identified by scholars that don't require outright annihilation in 117:

- The Ninth was moved out sometime after 108 to support deployments for the Eastern war, leaving only two legions in Britain. Such a major depletion would certainly have been a factor in any British revolt. This scenario postulates that the Sixth was moved in around 119-120 to suppress the troubles and bring the garrison back up to three legions, which by then was recognized as necessary and sufficient to hold Britain.
- The Ninth really was severely mauled in a British revolt. This is a reasonable possibility, but it doesn't have to involve disbandment or annihilation. Minus the 'Eagle factor' this is in fact

Sutcliff's narrative, since she has Guern the Hunter say that the expedition went out well under strength with detachments abroad. She never claims annihilation, only the loss of the principal officers and standard (and therefore disbandment).

And incidentally, we don't know that losing the Eagle necessarily entailed disbandment every time. It was always disgraceful and taken hard by the survivors, but what actually happened in any given instance was probably heavily driven by political factors. What we notice is that units seem to stop disappearing by the mid-third century, which is just when unit losses should have been heavy. A fairly reliable primary source, Dio Cassius, writing before 229, assures us that the Eagle 'is never moved from the winter-quarters (i.e., the base headquarters) unless the whole army takes the field'.[10] Why it didn't is pretty obvious. Politically, first-century Rome could afford to write off an Eagle or two. Third-century Rome had no such cushion.

If we accept the second version, we might also accept that post-117 the high command simply said, "That's

---

[10] The statement is made in an explanatory aside to his history of Crassus' defeat in 53 BCE but Dio tends to retroject usages from his own experience three centuries later. But you can't lose an Eagle that isn't out there with you, and by the third century, the Romans couldn't afford to lose any. The battlegroup system of assignments mentioned elsewhere, where a whole legion was almost never in the field at once, provided a useful political fig leaf.

three times in eighty years, time for a change of scene", sent them to the continent, and rotated *Victrix* in behind them. Some think they were lost in the Bar-Kochba rising of 132 in Judea. That revolt did apparently destroy one other legion, *XXII Deiotariana* from Egypt, and it could have seen the end of *Hispana* as well. Other conjectures place the end in Marcus Aurelius' Armenian war of around 161, when again we know that an unknown legion was destroyed. At any rate, by 165, the Ninth was history.

What about the famous Calleva Eagle, which helped inspire Sutcliff? It was found under the floor of the basilica at Calleva by the Reverend J. G. Joyce during his excavations in 1866. The eagle was found between two layers of burnt material. Joyce believed that the eagle was the imperial standard of a Roman legion. (Sutcliff tells the story of how it got from Uncle Aquila's house to the basilica in the sequel to *Eagle of the Ninth*, *The Silver Branch*).

It is Roman. It is an eagle. But it is increasingly less likely that it's a Roman Eagle. We now know that Roman Britain declined the basilica was used for metalworking, so the Eagle discovered there could simply have been a decorative item brought in for smelting.[11]

---

[11] No legionary Eagle has survived. This is hardly surprising since, allowing for losses and new creations post-27 BCE, there would only ever have been about 40 in existence up to about 285. A legion that had had an Eagle in 27 BCE would normally have had that same Eagle in 394 CE. The Battle of the Frigidus, 394 CE, is the last battle where the Eagles are said to have flown (on the Western side only), since

That's the history. What about the legend? The end of the Ninth in Britain or elsewhere is a legitimate historical mystery, but is it a legend in the true sense of the word?

The mystery was noticed as soon as Englishmen began to take an educated interest in their Roman past in the early eighteenth century. The antiquarian John Horsley writes in 1732 concerning the Ninth: "it might possibly be broke" (i.e., destroyed), but he had no answer. The question has preoccupied historians of Roman Britain ever since, and unless we find some really compelling new evidence, it's going to stay mysterious.[12]

As to legend, there are legends about Roman Britain, just as there are about the Germanic nations, that go deep into the past and are traceable to genuinely antique sources. The tales of King Arthur have their deepest literary roots in Gildas, who probably wrote in the early sixth century, and in the writings of the Venerable Bede of the early eighth. And the *Dream of Macsen Wledig* and its associated Celtic stories of the *Mabinogion* go farther back still, to the 380s, for Macsen Wledig was the great rebel general Magnus Maximus (from *Puck of Pook's Hill*),

---

thereafter they would have been cast down, destroyed and replaced by the Chi-Rho *labarum* of the Christian Empire.

The Eagle depicted on the front cover is a fine replica created by the re-enactor unit *X Gemina* (NL). It is faithful to the (very few) depictions in Roman sculpture.

[12] In 2011, Donald B. Campbell of the University of Glasgow's Continuing Education Department published a survey of the Ninth Legion in *Ancient Warfare*, to which I am greatly indebted for the present piece.

who failed to take over the Empire and died in 388. From about 383, he littered a collection of sub-Roman buffer kings in the north, from whom later Celtic rulers claimed descent. One of them—possibly—was *Coel Hen*, Coel the Old, in Latin, Coelius, who passed into nursery rhyme as Old King Cole.

But native sources don't go reliably farther back than that and they certainly don't mention the Ninth, two hundred and fifty years before. The oldest Teutonic myths from the Continent don't go beyond the death of Ermanaric the Ostrogoth in 375 or so. The *Nibelungenlied* has roots that go back at least to the fifth century. But the veritable Germanic descendants of Hermann 'the Liberator', slayer of Varus in 9, had no idea he'd ever existed until they learned to read their Tacitus.

Furthermore, legends of that vintage are guaranteed to be historically incoherent. Gildas never mentions Arthur by name; his literary successors were less restrained. Everybody threw something into the oral stew at one point or other before the legends were written down centuries after, usually around the tenth century, so we find Macsen Wledig contending with Brutus in some versions, and Kriemhild of Burgundy meeting up with Attila the Hun (*Etzel*) and Theoderic the Ostrogoth (*Dietrich of Bern*) in the *Nibelungenlied*. The great legends have a world of their own which is not of this world.

If there is a legend of the Ninth Legion, it begins only in 1954 but it seems to have grown roots. The movies would not have been made if it hadn't. One day perhaps the mystery will be solved by archaeology. In the meantime, as Thucydides reminds us, what we believe about our past can be more important than what really happened. We make legends because we need legends.

Mars still has its canals. Schiaparelli 'discovered' them, Edgar Rice Burroughs made them real, the Mars probes prove they're not there. They are real because somehow we need them to be, and somewhere in imagination they always will be, along with the Ninth and its Eagle.

Chapter Five

Peaceful Coexistence:
The Watch on the Rhine

As long as they're busy fighting each other, they're not fighting us.[1]

— *Tacitus, Germania*

When we think of the German peoples whom the Romans faced across the Rhine and Danube, aka the 'barbarians',[2] the image that usually comes to mind is a bunch of great hairy warriors (usually with horned helmets which the Vikings then somehow seem to have inherited)[3] somewhere 'out there', who periodically inundate the northern frontiers and sweep all before

---

[1] Tacitus actually said: *May the Gods continue and perpetuate amongst these nations, if not any love for us, yet by all means this their animosity and hate towards each other: since whilst the destiny of the Empire thus urges it, fortune cannot more signally befriend us, than in sowing strife amongst our foes.* Brevity was not one of his strong suits.

[2] Originally a Greek pejorative for everyone who didn't speak Greek; to them any other language sounded like *bar-bar-bar*.

[3] Neither Germans nor Vikings ever wore horned helmets. Not even on holidays. On the other hand, some Romans did—little wee ones seem to have been a badge of the staff adjutant post called *cornicularius*. Look hard at modern military insignia before snickering.

them—eventually contributing to the Fall of Rome. As usual, we can blame Hollywood for some misrepresentation—but not completely.

The stereotype, with roots in Roman cultural bias, was that the Germans were intractable savages living in a terrifying dank, misty wilderness and addicted to rapine, pillage, and associated national pastimes.[4] Tacitus in his *Germania*, published around 100 CE, describes small tribes and clans with elective kingships, mutable political alignments, and a pastoral way of life, with considerable military skills and a penchant for warfare. He contributes a great deal to the 'noble savage' stereotype that European culture has been addicted to on and off ever since, because the *Germania* is a lightly veiled and pointed contrast of German political liberty and Roman autocracy (Tacitus wrote under Trajan but had survived Domitian). It's the only 'sociological' monograph we have from the time and as far as we can tell, given cultural and ideological biases, it's not a bad one. At least it tells us what the Romans knew and thought of what was going on 'out there' at the turn of the second century. But there are five hundred years of history to account for, and the story is a great deal more complex.

---

[4] Lindsey Davis in her Falco, P.I. mystery *The Iron Hand of Mars* evokes the sense of haunted dread and vile deeds done that all good Romans were supposed to feel 'out there'. But the story is set only a year or so after the Civilis Revolt of 70 CE. The whole Rhineland would still have been traumatized. Marcus (*The Eagle of the Ninth*) Aquila's Caledonia is mysterious but nowhere near as menacing.

To begin (more or less) from the beginning: the Germanic peoples burst on Rome like a thunderclap in the last years of the second century BCE in the form of two migrating tribes, the Cimbri and Teutones, who destroyed a Roman army at Orange (*Arausio*)[5] in Provence in 105 BCE and then were destroyed by the Consul Marius in two battles, at Aix-en-Provence (*Aquae Sextiae*) in 102 and a northern Italian locality called *Vercellae* in 101. After having spent about two hundred and ninety years[6] dreading the Gauls (and wreaking pre-emptive retaliation on them at every opportunity), the Romans and Gauls now had a new common terror, the *furor Teutonicus*.

Forty-odd years later, in a convoluted political betrayal allegedly at the behest of the central Gallic tribes, Julius Caesar defeated the German leader Ariovistus,[7] who was a recognized 'friend and ally of the Senate and People of Rome' at the time and probably expected a little more consideration. Caesar crossed the

---

[5] The defeated proconsular Governor, Q. Servilius Caepio, gets a deservedly bad name in Colleen McCulloch's novel *The First Man in Rome*. He was also the grandfather of Julius Caesar's sometime girlfriend Servilia (HBO's *Rome*).

[6] Since the sacking of Rome by the Gallic leader Brennus in 389 BCE with his famous and probably apocryphal cry '*Vae victis*/Woe to the conquered'.

[7] Of the tribe of the Suebi. The Suebi were large, important, and around for the entire period of Roman-German relations. After Ariovistus, they appear to have gone back eastward, because in Imperial times they are living closer to the Elbe than the Rhine.

Rhine at Andernach, building a highly impressive timber bridge to do it, and then breaking it down after a brief foray. The whole exercise seems to have been a propaganda manouevre on the level of his two landings in Britain three and four years later—just to show he could do it. Vladimir Putin's adventure into Georgia in 2008 is reminiscent and the motives were probably not all that different. The politics of machismo have eternal qualities all their own.

Caesar's Gallic campaigns wrapped up in 49 BCE. What happened in Gaul over the next twenty-five years—the Civil Wars and immediately after—is not known in much detail, but with perhaps as many as 1.2 million Gallic dead over ten years not counting innumerably more sold into slavery, Gaul wasn't going anywhere for a generation or so. The surviving Gallic aristocracy made their peace in short order.[8]

By the 20s BCE at the latest, Rome was solidly established on the left bank of the Rhine. Both banks were inhabited by Germans. The definition of 'German' is neither more nor less indefinite than any modern ethnic monicker, especially in times of sovereignty referenda. However, the proto-German-speaking tribes of the left bank, including notably the Batavians in Holland, the Treveri around Trier (*Augusta Treverorum*, later an Imperial capital), and the Ubii

---

[8] The adopted *nomen* Julius is very prevalent in first-century Gaul. Its bearers could have been sponsored for citizenship by either Caesar himself or Augustus.

around Cologne[9] all seem to have taken to the benefits of Roman civilization like ducks to water. The Batavians in particular contributed nine auxiliary cohorts worth of amphibious infantry to the Imperial Army, within the Roman command structure but officered by their own nobles.[10] Judging by contemporary references, the Romans thought of them as 'special forces' and were highly proud of the relationship, as were the Batavians, who were tax-exempt as a result.

Augustus made a serious attempt at expansion into cross-Rhine Germany. The objective seems to have been to establish a frontier on the Elbe, which would have allowed for a vastly shortened frontier between the head of the Elbe and the Danube. It was not to be. The venture ended with the Varus disaster (*clades Variana*) of 9 CE at a location called the *Teutoburger Wald*. Three legions, *XVII*, *XVIII*, and *XIX*, were destroyed in an ambush set up by Hermann[11] 'the Liberator' of the tribe of the Cherusci. He had been a Roman Auxiliary officer in his time; comparisons could be drawn with Dzhokhar Dudayev,

---

[9] *Colonia Claudia Ara Agrippinensium Ubiorum*, capital of the military district of Lower Germany. It's doubtful that anyone waited for the barbarians to arrive before shortening the windier Roman place names.

[10] The most familiar analogue to the Batavian relationship would be the Gurkhas in British service. There are many more relationships of the sort down the centuries.

[11] Originally in Latin, '*Arminius*'. The battlefield has now been discovered near Kalkreise and is every bit as impressive as Tacitus tells it.

the rebel Chechen leader in the 1990s, who began life as a Soviet Air Force general. Hermann also seems to have been a highly efficient conspirator, and Varus by all accounts an unsuitable political appointment[12] completely asleep at the switch. Other family members of Hermann's remained loyal to Rome, and the feud split the tribe wide open.

There were several strong retaliatory expeditions in the decade following, under the Caesar Germanicus.[13] From then up to 85, the garrisons of Lower and Upper Germany were established at four legions each and there was little serious military activity on that frontier for many years.

Along the Rhine, water seems to have been thicker than blood; there was no love lost between the Germans of the opposing banks. When the Empire fissioned after Nero's assassination in 68 and the Year of Three Emperors distracted Roman attention and troops from the Rhine sector, the Batavians under a leading noble named Julius Civilis rebelled and were joined by some of the northern Gauls.

But it doesn't seem to have been a 'nationalist' rebellion. Civilis may have had ideas, but Tacitus says that the affair began with a (probably justifiable) personal

---

[12] His previous postings had been Africa and Syria, both of which he is said to have governed very harshly. He had been Governor of Germany for three years, which seems to have been enough time for feelings to fester and the revolt to gather steam.

[13] The Emperor Tiberius' nephew, well-known to all readers and viewers of Robert Graves' *I, Claudius*.

and tribal grievance and then spread as the Empire fell further into brief instability. When the tribes from across the Rhine decided to get into the act they were not fraternally embraced.[14]

When the civil strife of 69-70 was over and the experienced general Petilius Cerialis showed up with eight legions, most of the rebellion collapsed. Contrary to Rome's historic reputation (and to what was going on in Judaea at the time), there were no bloody mass reprisals. Cerialis, probably on instructions from his cousin the new Emperor Vespasian, was ready to deal. On hearing that Jerusalem had finally fallen, Civilis seems to have negotiated a capitulation, accepted a hefty buy-out, and disappeared from history. The Batavians went back to providing an essential element of the Army, still with their own officers,[15] but geographically reassigned to reduce temptation.

Around 85 the Romans occupied a district called the *Agri Decumates* ('Ten Cantons') in the Upper Rhine — Upper Danube acute angle between Mainz in the northwest and just west of Regensburg in the southeast. It seems to have been already Romanized and after annexation was heavily defended by a

---

[14] The good citizens of Cologne are said to have invited their not-too-distant relations over to a big reconciliation banquet and burned the hall down over the lot of them.

[15] One of them shows up at the famous British site of Vindolanda near the line of Hadrian's Wall in about 100 CE with the telltale name of Flavius Cerialis, commanding the Ninth Batavians. Most likely his father had been sponsored by Petilius for exceptional loyalty during the revolt and, as customary, taken Vespasian's clan name Flavius.

garrisoned overland rampart and ditch (the *Limes Germanicus*) with forts on which the more elaborate Hadrian's Wall in Britain was later based. This shortened the lines of communication between the Rhine and the Danube, where the Emperor Domitian was beginning to have serious trouble. The Dacian kingdom (in Rumania) destroyed at least one legion (Julius Caesar's *V Alaudae*) in 86 and the whole centre of gravity on the northern frontier pivoted from Rhine to Danube forever.

The Danube commitment caused the immediate halting of Agricola's (over-ambitious) offensive operations in northern Britain. It also led to the draw-down of the Rhine garrisons by a startling fifty percent, to two legions in each of upper and lower Germany. Domitian's judgement was sound; the Rhine frontier caused no significant problems for—amazingly—nearly a hundred and thirty years.

More than a century is a long period in which relationships can build up. They need not always be *friendly* relationships, but coexistence is very possible, especially in a society where ethnic differences mattered far less than social or economic ones, as was the case with Rome and most of her near neighbours. There is growing evidence that the Germans on the right bank (the ones who had destroyed Varus) gradually developed into a settled society and that their nobles came more and more to enjoy and emulate Roman material lifestyles after their own fashion. They weren't reading Vergil, but they had villas,[16] perhaps a few imported cooks, certainly household goods—and armaments.[17] There was occasional legislation against selling arms across the frontier but it seems to have had as little effect as current export-control legislation does (and probably many a retired centurion supplemented his income in the munitions trade).[18] Roman manufactured

---

[16] There was more sophisticated construction around Germany than we usually give credit for. Herodian, whom we will meet again in Chapter Six, notes their skill in timber construction: *Although there is a scarcity of stone and fired brick in Germany, the forests are dense, and timber is so abundant that they build their houses of wood, fitting and joining the squared beams.* Considering that their culture evolved the Viking long ship, we should probably not be surprised.

[17] There are rich finds of Roman-manufactured goods in Denmark. Interestingly, there are also finds of Roman-pattern weapons that seem to have been made in Scandinavia.

[18] There is a second-century inscription from Slovakia: *interprex legionis XV idem centurio negotiator* which translates freely as 'interpreter and procurement centurion for Legion XV'. *XV Apollinaris* shuttled between the Middle Danube and the Eastern military sectors during the first century. There is a second-century inscription from Mainz referring to a *negotiator gladiarius*, 'dealer in swords', presumably with a licence.

It is not hard to imagine a centurion with regional liaison responsibilities taking his pension and going on to 'make his money' (as the Americans put it) doing exactly what he'd been doing in uniform for the past ten years. Even this may be too 'constructed' an interpretation; the line between civil and military was probably pretty fuzzy at any time. My thanks to Dr. Bishop and Mr. Roger Lucy for their advice and information on this activity. Dr. Bishop points out

goods made their way to the Baltic and beyond (Autobahn 7 from Mainz northeastward was one of the major trade arterials).

Just as significant is the growing body of evidence for mutual trade in what we call 'commodities'. There seem to have been iron mines all through Germany as far as present-day Poland, and the sector garrisons themselves very probably procured a lot of their provisions from across the river.[19]

They also procured human resources. From the earliest days of the relationship, no German father would have thought anything of sending his surplus sons off to join the Army and see the world (Hermann set a bad example that most didn't follow). No recruiting centurion would have thought anything of taking them. And if they never came home but settled outside the base in Syria with a Spanish wife and kids, they and the Empire both had the best of the deal.

Later writers would spend much ink and energy decrying 'barbarization' of the Army, but what we have here is not *barbarization* in any sense that is a threat to the status quo, Juvenal to the contrary notwithstanding.[20] Very

---

that all the known *negotiatores* are from the Upper Rhine and Danube, which suggests that there was a lot of business there to be done.

[19] Peter S. Wells, *The Barbarians Speak: How the Conquered Peoples Shaped Roman Europe* (2001) summarizes the known extent of development beyond the frontiers. More is being discovered.

[20] *Satires* 3: *Syrian Orontes has long since flowed into the Tiber, and brought with it its language, morals, and the crooked harps with the flute-player* and so on. Meanwhile Flavius Cerialis, the Ninth Batavians'

likely over much of the period, the Army would simply contact a few of the friendlier chiefs in the vicinity when they needed a draft of likely-looking youngsters,[21] some of whom might have been taught a few things by their elders who had already served. During hostilities, rounding up hordes of draftees was a regular practice, as we will see.

Nonetheless, demography was having its say. The Roman frontier was a barrier to movement where none had existed before. Population density in western and southern Germany was building.

This showed most obviously in the coalescence of tribes into federations. It started earliest in the south, what is now Bavaria and the Czech lands, where the federation of the Marcomanni ('Border-men') was already in existence under Tiberius.[22] He and Claudius

---

commander's son, might have been holding an Imperial commission defending Juvenal and friends from whatever really might trouble them, and with lots of boys from over the Rhine in his command— speaking and writing Latin.

[21] This may have been one of the duties of the Regional Centurions. A scene in the Praetorium at Cologne: *Have you got that draft of men I was looking for from the Tencteri? They what? Want to renegotiate the provisioning agreement again? Hercules' rupture, now I have to have Sigimer and his idiots over to dinner again. Send them the invitation and make sure they find the bathhouse this time.* Arms-running profits no doubt made up for this sort of casual abuse.

[22] Fascinatingly, the Marcomanni included the Boii, a Celtic tribe whom the Republic had encountered, and one that seems to have wandered all over south central Europe, happily bequeathing its name to Bavaria and Bohemia.

fought a few desultory wars with them, then bought them off.

Foreign aid has always been 'tied' to commercial or political leverage and the Romans were experts at it, as were their Byzantine descendants. We have only the foggiest glimpses of it, but the relationship between Rome and its neighbours in Germany and Britain always was based on a dynamic-balance arrangement kept intact by favours and gifts here, a demonstration of force there, and trade always and everywhere. One researcher, Lynn Pitts, has noted that with the larger and stronger polities such as the Marcomanni, the policy seems to have been: trade, political recognition, subsidies as required, but never direct military support.[23]

This is a policy that has emerged throughout history when a large power becomes neighbours with many smaller bordering powers, some of whom are nonetheless strong enough to either render it assistance

---

[23] Lynn S. Pitts, "Relations Between Rome and the German 'Kings' on the Middle Danube in the First to Fourth Centuries A.D.", *Journal of Roman Studies* 1989. Pitts also notes that in the first century the Marcomanni are said to have disposed of seventy thousand infantry and four thousand cavalry. Troop strengths now or then are very slippery and subject to inflation. Those numbers may have been what King Maroboduus thought he could call up but it is not very likely that he could have fielded an expeditionary force of that size. (By comparison, the Russians in March 2014 were said to have mobilized up to sixty thousand troops on the border of Ukraine from an army of nearly three hundred thousand). In any case, it would be far too strong a force for the Romans to have tolerated.

or do it harm. As we saw in Chapter Two, the Imperial government ran a very tight military budget. Seven brigaded legions held the Rhine and Upper Danube at most times, and they were only sufficient if backed by an active diplomacy. The border zones were permeable, and it would have been a rare annual conference at the Governor's HQ where some Legate did not say to another—in the bathhouse, very quietly after a drink or two—*'if those beggars come into my sector this year I am SO screwed...'* Eventually, that happened.

Marcus Aurelius, 170s: 'Germany and Sarmatia' Collection of Mr. Roger Lucy

Somewhere between 167 and 170 under the great and long-suffering Emperor Marcus Aurelius, the dam broke in the north. The Marcomanni and Quadi suddenly swamped the Danube defences and got almost to the head of the Adriatic before being repulsed, despite there having been serious fighting in the sector since 166, and the Roman military consequently being in a state of alertness.[24] We do not know why this should have happened when it did. Since 166 there had been a major plague sweeping the Empire with catastrophic impact on economic and military strength. The Romans didn't see the attack coming—a disastrous

---

[24] We also don't know exactly when between 166 and 170 it happened, which makes analysis more than a little murky.

failure of intelligence[25]—and it took ten years to drive the tribes back across the Danube. Marcus was preparing to create two new trans-Danubian provinces in the current Czech Republic and western Hungary when he died in 180. His son Commodus abandoned the annexation effort.[26]

After the Marcomannic Wars we see a trend whereby the Romans try to negotiate 'no man's lands' of unpopulated areas close to their frontiers, and tightly regulate the timing and location of contacts. This does not seem to have worked all that well. By the fourth

---

[25] At least one book on Roman intelligence (*Exploratio: Military & Political Intelligence in the Roman World*, by N. J. E. Austin and N. B. Rankov, 1995) had its start when a senior professor asked its authors: 'What I want to know is, did the Governor have a filing cabinet marked "intelligence"?'

He may not have had quite that Rome organized its bureaucracy on different lines than ours. But the two sides knew each other well, and at least for an offensive operation (Chapter Six) the Governor had access to knowledgeable local sources—'humint', either as political intelligence or guides and scouts on the ground. (In that period, 'sigint'—signals intelligence—would at best have consisted of finding the message capsule before eating the pigeon.) As in this case, Governors could also have disastrous failures, probably most often on the defensive. With only humint to go on, knowing what's 'out there' in general terms is far easier than finding out exactly what may be coming at you—but not all that easy anyway. That is true even today. Defensive intelligence must be proactive but depends a lot on lucky breaks—and you can't know for certain until the shooting starts. Vladimir Putin is highly skilled at exploiting this blind spot.

[26] As depicted in *Gladiator* (2000). It may have been a rational decision reflecting differences of opinion in Marcus' council.

century, advanced fortifications at bridgeheads seem to have become the order of the day, and on the middle Danube there are indications of possibly more elaborate fortifications on the far side of the river.

The trend toward tribal federation seems to have started in the south—the Marcomannic lands—and slowly percolated northwards along the Rhine. Similar fusion processes were happening. By 200 at latest, a federation called the Alemanni ('*All-men*') had come into existence in the middle Rhine. Later in the same century, a third federation, the Franks (which might mean '*Free-men*', or might not), arose on the northernmost stretch of the frontier above Cologne. (One current theory suggests that the Goths, who appear in the mid-third century, are products of a similar process on the Lower Danube.)

Eastward from these three groupings were what we know loosely as the East Germans, who include the Suebi and other later-to-be famous names: the Lombards, the Vandals, the Burgundians, the Saxons. As we have seen, the Suebi had had relationships with the Romans since at least Caesar's day.

What is notable, and has been noted for a long time, is that when the dismemberment of the Western provinces finally happened in the early fifth century, it was the East German peoples who were its principal agents. They moved through the Alemannic and Frankish lands and flooded into Gaul and Spain in the first decade of the fifth century while the Goths did the same on the Lower Danube and in Provence/Aquitaine. But not one of those wandering peoples left a modern

European legacy. That was the heritage of the Franks, who moved very slowly into France, and the Alemanni who essentially stayed put in western Germany. Those who had been longest and closest in contact with Rome became her successors; those farther removed, her destroyers.[27]

One thing more stands out: that although cultural and economic life in Germany was more complex than traditionally assumed, there was still a big difference between Out and In. If you were a German, great or humble, the Empire was where you wanted to be.[28] The process accelerated to the point where in the fourth century, Constantine the Great began the trend of promoting first-generation Germans into command positions. This caused a great deal of nationalist animosity in court circles at the time, growing greater as Rome's troubles grew, but in fact as far as we can tell, none of these men ever showed the least sign of disloyalty to the culture they had adopted and the polity they served. The Goths who destroyed a Roman army in 378 and finally sacked Rome in 410 were acting as free agents, under the fig leaf of Roman service, and not under effective training,

---

[27] The exception to the rule is the Angles, Saxons, and Jutes, who were able to take over the Roman province of Britain.

[28] At one point a certain category of them who seem to have got land grants as well came to be called *laeti* (very possibly meaning 'the happy campers' in regional centurions' jargon) because they got the big prize: life in the Empire. The current situation on the US/Mexican border bears certain resemblances though it is doubtful that Roman-German immigration questions were usually so politically charged.

discipline, or control. Here is when the phrase *barbarization of the Army* can at last be sanctioned.

The difference in standards of living lasted to the very end of the West. From at least 350 onward, eastern Gaul came more and more under threat of raids from across the Rhine. Yet the poet Ausonius could write his *Mosella*, describing the placid and prosperous rural life of the Moselle valley, perhaps around 380,[29] Trier was an Imperial capital until about 390, with monuments that today are second only to Rome and Istanbul among Imperial capitals, and right up to the last day of 406, when the East Germans swarmed across the frozen Rhine, a life of luxury was lived in the villas along the left bank.[30]

A half century or so later the Franks were stabling their horses in the roofless throne room of the Imperial Palace at Trier, the *aula palatina*. Today, following the fire-bombing of 1944, it is a gloriously restored archaeological monument and Evangelical church—but in the fifth century there was no Marshall Plan.

---

[29] He does mention new fortifications and a not-very-old battlefield.

[30] In February 2014, a spectacular hoard dating from about 406 was found within a few miles of the Rhine at Rülzheim near Speyer, so rich it has been sensationally (and egregiously) linked to the legendary treasure of the Nibelungs (with thanks to Bild.de via Adrian Murdoch, Bread and Circuses blog, http://adrianmurdoch.typepad.com/my_weblog/).

Chapter Six

Familiar Territory:
A Surge into Germany

...had not all the Germans fled to the swamps and forests, he would have brought all Germany under Roman sway.

—*Herodian*

The middle fifty years of the third century of this era were not the best half-century Rome ever experienced. In fact they might have been about the worst. Military coups, barbarian invasions, hyperinflation, and on top of all else an endemic plague. By 260 CE the Empire had split into three parts and it was only put together again by brilliant efforts founded on some real sentiments of self-interested patriotism coalescing in the Army of the Danube.

But traditional scholarship has always assumed that if things got that bad that fast after 235, they must have been in pretty bad shape already. The Army had been barbarized, degraded; sources speak of the rapacity of the soldiers, the greed of the soldiers, the demands of the soldiers.[1] There was some of that to be sure. The

---

[1] There were 'issues of discipline' at various times. There were also what we would now call 'labour-related issues' which could likewise be fatal to the Emperor who encountered them. There were also garden-variety coups or putsches (guideline: if the Guards do it—

Army was becoming more and more an independent social and political force in the Empire, as the Emperors were becoming more and more beholden to it,[2] and then as now, an Army with its own corporate agenda is never a good idea.

In 2000, just outside the town of Kalefeld, Lower Saxony, two hobbyists with metal detectors were exploring an undistinguished ridge called the Harzhorn overlooking an ancient trade route from the Rhine to the Baltic called Autobahn 7. What they found was probably not what they were looking for, but buried mediaeval treasure pales by comparison. It was

---

usually in Rome—it's a coup. If the Command Staff in Theatre does it, it's a putsch). Quite a few of the third-century changes of Emperor often loosely attributed to 'the soldiers' seem to have been command putsches.

But there were also class and cultural issues. Dio Cassius, writing around 229, gets very grumpy because after the civil war of 193 the Praetorian Guard, which had been locally recruited from good Italian boys, was replaced by troops promoted from the frontier armies, resulting in *a throng of motley soldiers most savage in appearance, most terrifying in speech, and most boorish in conversation*. Dio also mentions the impact of the move on Italian unemployment in the youth demographic; he intuitively grasped the concept of the Guard as social safety net. Dio, as we have seen already, was no slouch as an analyst.

[2] On his deathbed in 211 in Britain, Septimius Severus, whose rule was based in an 'empowered' military, told his sons Caracalla and Geta, 'Stick together, pay the Army, and to hell with the rest of them'. It was good advice in the circumstances, sixty-six percent adhered to in the event.

a Roman cavalry horseshoe[3] of a pattern known to have been used in the third century.

They waited until 2008 to show it to Dr. Petra Lönne, an archaeologist at the local museum in Kalefeld, who then mobilized every volunteer with a metal detector in the area. Over the next two years they discovered over fifteen hundred artifacts from a Roman/German battlefield of the middle of the third century.

They found coins. The earliest, very worn, ones were from the Emperor Commodus (180-192). The latest, quite crisp, ones were late issues from the reign of Alexander Severus (222-235). That dates the battle to (probably) the year 235 in the reign of the very short-lived Emperor Maximinus Thrax (235-238).

The shock of the moment was that, based on all modern scholarship, no such battlefield should have existed. For most of the modern era it was an article of faith that after their disastrous defeat beyond the Rhine under Varus in 9,[4] the Romans never again penetrated deeply into Germany. But Kalefeld is very deep, about 250 kilometres toward the Elbe from the Rhine at

---

[3] A *hipposandal* (modern term). Horseshoe-shaped horseshoes were a mediaeval invention.

[4] The Varus disaster was the subject of an obsessive German national quest for years under the Kaisers and after. It was finally discovered in the early 1990s near the town of Kalkreise in North Rhine–Westphalia, and the remains—including the prepared German ambush sites—make clear that the first-century historians have left us an accurate account of an overwhelming disaster.

Mainz.[5] The Harzhorn discoveries also made it clear that the Romans were heading *homeward* from somewhere farther out when the action occurred. And it was a Roman victory.

Former US Secretary of War Donald Rumsfeld once said:

> *There are known knowns; there are things we know that we know. There are known unknowns; that is to say, there are things that we now know we don't know. But there are also unknown unknowns—there are things we do not know we don't know.*

That got him laughed at at the time but there is nothing wrong with the logic. Philosopher and cultural critic Slavoj Žižek has added a fourth category: *unknown knowns*—things that we ought to know perfectly well but somehow didn't notice. It is an *unknown known* that made the discovery of what is now known as 'the Battle at the Harzhorn' such a shock.

Contemporary sources are very imperfect where they exist at all. Texts can be confused in transcription and most copies of anything have gaps and variations. They can also be hard to penetrate because they are far less detailed than a modern history and the writers' ideas of source confirmation were very different from ours, even when the source is actually trying to write history as we know it. Roman

---

[5] *Mogontiacum* in those days, headquarters of the military district of Upper Germany.

readers seem to have preferred gossip, moral lessons, and colour—in other words, 'edutainment'. Faking sources wasn't unheard of. It doesn't help that most mediaeval copyists had no sense of context for what they were copying.

For the period 230-240 there is one fairly decent contemporary source named Herodian of Antioch, and then there's one written (probably) in the late fourth century called the *Historia Augusta*—the *Lives of the Later Caesars*—that ranks right down with the worst of them. It does have some reliable content cribbed from older sources. The trouble is, with only two extant sources, the opportunity for cross-check is so slim that you can rarely know which unsupported sections of the *Lives* may actually have any worth. It's been known for centuries that large pieces of them are bogus. As we become more experienced with what is flying around social media, this should shock us rather less than it did earlier students of Classics.

An enjoyable example of the problems a source like the *Historia Augusta* poses: from the *Life of Aurelian* (270-275), we are given a marching song (the Historia calls it a dance) which—in a translation by Edgar Allan Poe, no less—goes:

> *A thousand, a thousand, a thousand,*
> *A thousand, a thousand, a thousand,*
> *We, with one warrior, have slain!*
> *A thousand, a thousand, a thousand,*
> *Sing a thousand over again!*
> *So ho!—let us sing*

Long life to our king,
Who knocked over a thousand so fine!
So ho!—let us roar,
He has given us more
Red gallons of gore
Than all Syria can furnish of wine!

Followed later by:

...A thousand Sarmatians, a thousand Franks
Now bring us a thousand Persians!

This has 'truthiness', or as a Victorian would have said, 'verisimilitude'. The time, place and context (274) are credible. Roman soldiers did sing marching songs (which they would add verses to as required) and Roman popular culture in general seems to have enjoyed mass singing. But did Aurelian's men really sing this song about him...? 'No external verification'.

Every once in a while archaeology hands us a major surprise, and we find that the ancients were telling no more than the truth.

Concerning the Emperor Maximinus Thrax's campaign across the Rhine, probably in 235 CE, the *Historia* says:

He marched...into Germany across the Rhine, and throughout three or four hundred miles of the barbarians' country he burned villages...

'Three or four hundred miles' seems plain enough. But in 1620 the French scholar Claude de Saumaise saw that phrase while preparing a new edition of the *Historia*, and seems to have said to himself, 'that can't be right, we know they couldn't get that far into Germany, has to be a mistranscription' and arbitrarily changed the phrase to 'thirty or forty'. Most subsequent assumptions about Roman–German relations have been based on that one editor's blunder.

Not only was the Roman Army of the third century fully capable of a major offensive into Germany, not only has a supposedly worthless source been proven correct, but we are pointed toward a whole new picture of what was really 'out there' and how well the Romans were acquainted with it.

The Harzhorn finds represent only the third ancient open-site battlefield ever found (the others are the Varus disaster at Kalkreise in 9 CE, and an encounter between Romans and Batavians in the Civilis Revolt of 69 CE at Krefeld-Gellep/*Gelduba*). And they have allowed a pretty accurate picture of the battle itself to be developed. They have also caused great debate among archaeologists because, when it comes down to it, what they have to work with is a debris field on a slope. Some highly reputable archaeologists have questioned whether the arrangement of the bits and pieces is an accurate indication of what happened that day in 235.[6]

---

[6] Archaeologists are very careful about caveatting their interpretations (often after too many encounters with the popular media). But the ground seems to have been undisturbed enough

But even if the assumed narrative turns out to be different, the finds themselves, pretty securely dated to Maximinus Thrax and his offensive of 235, tell us a lot that we didn't know about the Rome and the Germany of the day.

Among the other significant finds on the field[7] are:

- A carpentry axe and legionary's shovel.
- Some cart parts (bits of harness) on the lower base of the spur.
- An entrenching pickaxe (*dolabra*)[8] in magnificent shape with the name of the legion *IV Flavia* on it—the only unit identifier found so far. *IV Flavia* was based at Belgrade[9] which lends credibility to the sources' statement that it was a large expeditionary force.
- Dozens of spearheads, including one identifiably German one (with gold decoration; Roman spearheads were expendable and so undecorated).

---

through subsequent history that they can say with confidence that the artefacts were found where they fell in 235. Archaeologists rarely get to dig an undisturbed site, and far more rarely an open battlefield. It eliminates a lot of reference points and benchmarks that a 'normal' dig relies on like ramparts and structures. Archaeology, like paleontology, is a moving target.

[7] There is a full collection of photos from the dig at the English- and German-language Wikipedia sites for the battle. Search for 'Battle at the Harzhorn'.

[8] Historians have noted that the Roman *dolabra* is frighteningly identical to the postwar British Army pickaxe of identical design function. 'If it's not broken...'

[9] *Singidunum.*

- Two *pilum* (standard heavy infantry javelin) heads, confirming that the classic weapon was still in use by the legions.
- A piece of a Roman cavalry helmet of known third-century pattern, and a chunk of very fine chainmail, of unknown ownership. Many types of Roman troops wore chainmail, as did any German noble who could afford it, so all we can be sure of is that if it's chainmail, it came from a Roman workshop. The peak and the mail are the only items of personal equipment found to date. No swords. No shields. There are almost no personal items and no human remains. It is one *clean* battlefield, although Dr. Bishop stresses that all battlefields discovered so far are like this; metal was simply too precious not to recycle. Finding so many missile heads where they fell almost certainly means that the Romans were in a hurry.
- A trail of hobnails (bootnails)[10] up the slope of the spur on the north side, marking the line of the infantry's advance. It is a straight path in the direction they were going, and it suggests that the infantry at least may never have deployed from column to line of battle.

---

[10] Most of us now have never worn a nailed sole, let alone a classic hobnailed soldier's boot. The soles were pretty well solid metal studding, slippery as the dickens on any kind of pavement, and the nails were liable to pop out frequently. As Dr. Bishop notes, almost all ancient military kit was very high-maintenance.

And most significantly:
- Windrows of arrowheads and artillery (*scorpion*) bolts, arranged to suggest a semicircular field of fire around the eastward base of the spur.

The *scorpio*[11] is the light two-armed torsion-powered infantry catapult illustrated in Chapter Two, made of wood and metal, sometimes with an ornamented gunshield and either a tripod or a light two-wheeled field carriage. It shot three-foot bolts, had a crew of two, and there were notionally fifty-five of them per legion.

The military college of the German Army has a classical warfare section and during 2012 and 2013, they were out on the Harzhorn slope doing scientific firing experiments with reconstructed scorpions. Despite the impression that a couple of breathless articles in the German media may have created, the capacities of the weapon have been well-known for decades,[12] but the research has confirmed that the rate of fire (using only the modern college student) is up to

---

[11] The nomenclature of ancient artillery is confusing, not least because that which the learned scholar called *ballista* (because it threw things), the gunnery centurion may have called *scorpio* (because it stung things). Terminology also mutated over the centuries.

[12] Classical artillery and technology pioneer Dr. Eric W. Marsden (*Greek and Roman Artillery*, 1969) once almost annihilated the entire Classics Department of Carleton University in Ottawa with a single misfire in the early 1980s. Your author witnessed this. They say that for decades after there was a scorpion bolt in the ceiling of the auditorium.

five rounds a minute (which means a trained crew could probably have got seven).[13] It has confirmed that the muzzle velocity is stupefying,[14] and that properly deployed they could create a true kill zone. Seventy-four bolts were found in an area the size of a dining room on the Harzhorn field. They legitimately occupied the technological and operational niche of a machine gun section in an early twentieth-century army, and a reasonable supposition is that they did deploy in sections.

The big discovery in the tests is that humidity doesn't affect them. Wetness makes any kind of natural bowstring go limp. But the big sinew skeins in the catapults performed just as well in pouring rain—an all-weather weapon.

The Harzhorn wasn't a major battle.[15] It doesn't seem to have involved more than a couple of thousand a side, but it is highly unlikely that anyone in their right mind would send only a couple of thousand men that deep into Germany, so what we seem to have is a clearing action in front of a much larger column. (The sources also suggest a large expeditionary force.)

---

[13] The Romans experimented from time to time with a hopper feed. It never worked properly and probably wasn't needed.

[14] Media reports don't mention the velocity, but apparently when they shot at a pig half, it burned the flesh on entry.

[15] There actually was a major battle, apparently in a very wet swamp, probably on the outward leg. Casualties on both sides are said to have been heavy, and the Emperor is said to have been so far out in front he got bogged down and had to be pulled out.

The Surge of 235

Peace on the Rhine was breached in 213 when the Alemanni attacked into the Ten Cantons district and the province of Raetia (south Bavaria). The Emperor Caracalla (Septimius Severus' elder son) waged a brief campaign for which we only have a propaganda notice.

A far more serious breach occurred in 233 under the young Emperor Alexander Severus, last of his (heavily Syrian) dynasty. The Alemanni again swamped the *limes*, and this time the damage was substantial. But the Empire's major problem at that point was strategic. They were looking at the horrifying prospect of a two-theatre war.[16]

In Chapter Three we left Mesopotamia newly under the control of a highly aggressive Sassanian Persian dynasty. The new King of Kings, Ardashir I, set out to restore the 'glory that was Persia', and he and his successor Shapur I (ca. 240-270) nearly destroyed Roman power in the East.

In 231-233 Alexander Severus was in Syria fighting a not-very-successful (and very costly) offensive against Ardashir when word came of the Alemannic attack. He hastily shifted the Army's centre of gravity back to the West, bringing many Eastern troops—cavalry and archers—with him, and prepared a massive attack into

---

[16] No state in history ever willingly fought a two-front land war except Nazi Germany which is probably the exception that proves the rule. To illustrate the point, the US was so overcommitted to the First Gulf War of 1991 that it could not have found deployable resources for another major commitment elsewhere.

Germany based on Mainz.[17] The word 'surge' has relevance because the intention was not to occupy, but to stabilize and suppress. The high command was intensely aware that the Eastern theatre had been left in a very unstable condition and that Ardashir would come at them again as soon as he could (as indeed he did).

The expeditionary force was ramped up—and Alexander unexpectedly decided to negotiate. A red line is a red line in any age, and Alexander had drawn one, then backed down. The sources tell us that he was far too much under the thumb of his mother, Julia Mammaea, and that 'the soldiers' wished for a stronger Emperor. The simplified narrative probably reflects genuine divisions of opinion in the high command going well beyond the Emperor's tent. For one thing Rome may have felt more threatened by the Alemanni than by Ardashir, but the Imperial Family had very deep personal connections 'out East'. What is very interesting is that the possibility of paying off the Alemanni seems to have been considered a feasible option in the policy toolkit by an influential faction in the command.

Consideration didn't last long. Severus and his mother were assassinated in a generals' putsch in early 235. He was replaced by a very experienced, very large,[18] and very lower-class general officer called Maximinus Thrax

---

[17] Herodian notes that Germany, being 'right next door' to Italy, was a far greater perceived threat than anything happening in the East.

[18] Eight Roman feet, six Roman inches. In English feet that's still eight foot three or 264 cm.

who was in command of the newly raised *Legio IV Italica* at the time.[19]

Maximinus had to suppress two counter-putsches (at least one originating from the Eastern troops) before he could march, but was probably moving by summer of 235.[20]

Herodian then says:

> *Maximinus led out his entire army and crossed the bridge fearlessly, eager to do battle with the Germans. Under his command was a vast number of men, virtually the entire Roman military force, together with many Moorish javelin men and Osrhoenian [eastern] and Armenian archers...*
>
> *...The javelin men and archers seemed to be especially effective against the Germans, taking them by surprise, attacking with agility and then retreating without difficulty.*
>
> *...Maximinus advanced deep into German territory, carrying off booty and turning over to the army all the herds they encountered.*

---

[19] There is some modern confusion about what unit of recruits he was commanding but it seems clear from *Historia Augusta* that it was the newly raised *IV Italica*.

[20] You can't keep a major force concentrated for very long in those logistical—let alone political—conditions. Even a modern force has problems doing that. Supplying NATO in Afghanistan over a twelve-year war only looked invisible from the outside. It was anything but. Keeping a major army eating in Mainz for more than a few weeks would have stretched the logistics system to the breaking point. Russia has been having similar problems with its forces on the Ukrainian border.

The *Historia Augusta* adds:

> ...*he burned villages, drove away flocks, slew numbers of the barbarians themselves, enriched his own soldiers, and took a host of captives, and, had not all the Germans fled to the swamps and forests, he would have brought all Germany under Roman sway.*

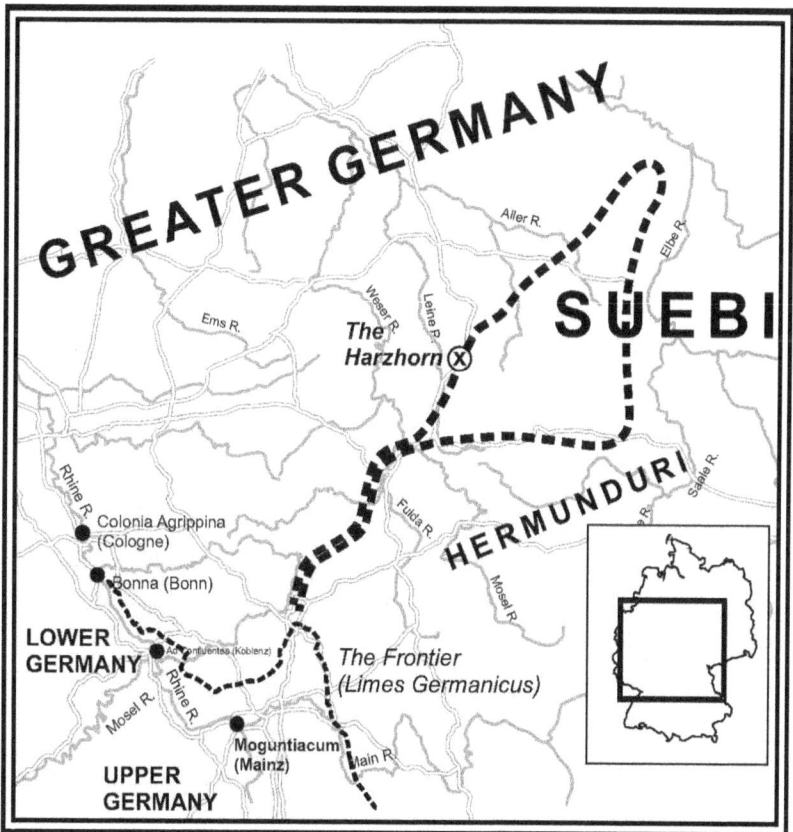

Projected line of march of Maximinus' column, 235 CE Kieran McAuliffe, after Braunschweiger Landesmuseum.

Now that we have located a battlefield, and we know that this particular action was fought on the return leg of the expedition, we can make some inferences from the sources.

- It was a big force. We don't know how big, but you would not want to go that deep into hostile territory with much under fifteen thousand troops and some estimates go as high as forty thousand. By this time mixed-element legionary battlegroups are the operational norm, so there's no knowing how many units might have been represented. The presence of *IV Flavia* elements from Belgrade suggests a wide draw.

On the other hand you couldn't supply many more than twenty thousand unless the land was very well settled. The Army seems to have been marching light, living off the land without its usual depot-and-convoy logistics—logical in the absence of roads. That is the significance of the *all the herds they encountered* reference by Herodian. Cattle don't make good booty because they're too hard to move. They were feeding the column on the fly.

- The Romans had much better and more detailed intelligence of conditions much farther 'out' than most study to date has recognized. The column clearly knew what it was looking for and found it.
- The expedition was probably also doing a lot of recruiting. The historian's 'captive' may easily be the Prefect's 'recruit'. A monument of Persian

King Shapur's from a few years later (around 244) brags about the vast number of 'Germans and Goths' that the Roman Army brought east—and Shapur captured.

- The Germans were fighting classic asymmetric warfare. The Romans seem to have been pleasantly surprised at how effective their light troops and archers were. When an organization is already over five hundred years old, it has to keep re-learning techniques.[21] They weren't worried about a quagmire because they weren't planning on staying (i.e., they had an exit strategy, as they too often did not in the East).

It is conjectured that the column went on a wide sweep east of Autobahn 7 on the outward leg, passing through the rich and well-populated Suebian country all the way to the Elbe. It then took the old trade route straight back, racing against its provisions. About a third of the distance to the *limes*—and we don't know where they had pitched camp the evening before—the Harzhorn came into view.

---

[21] For instance, how to fight elephants. The Army of the Republic could whip its weight in elephants every time, but they probably never saw another one until around 350 CE. By then, not surprisingly, they'd forgotten.

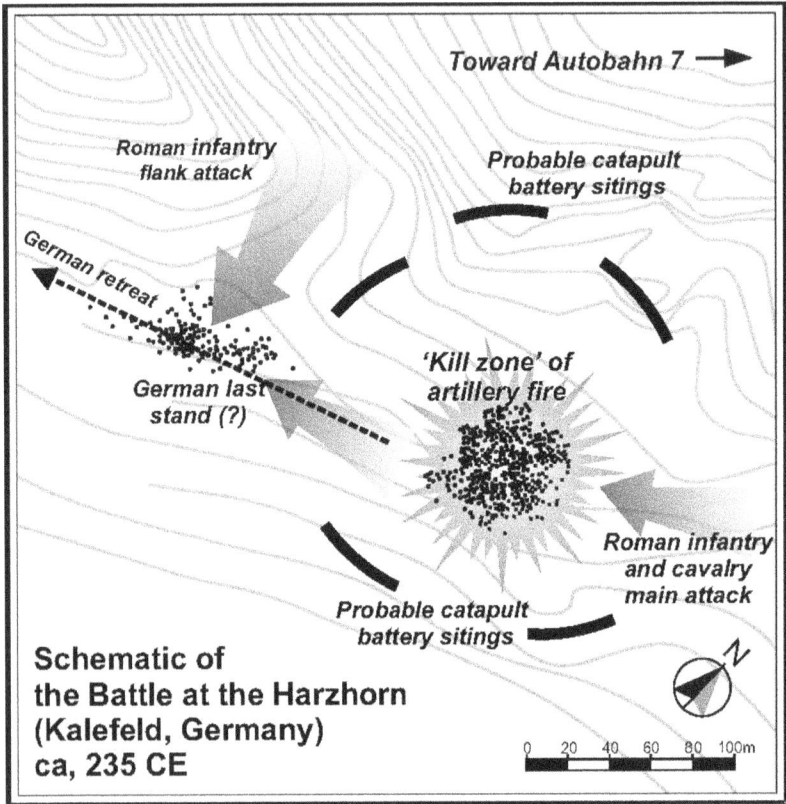

Schematic of the Harzhorn, showing artillery kill zone and probable battery sites.

Apocrypha II: The Action at the Harzhorn

What then happened is informed speculation based on the distribution pattern of about fifteen hundred bits and pieces, as interpreted by some very good archaeologists. But it might have unfolded this way:

> *I was up with the command group for a lot of the homeward leg. We're headed south a couple of hours out*

124

from camp, it's getting on for noon, and this ridge heaves into sight. We're following the track toward the gap on the left, and all of a sudden the ridge is infested.

I dunno what they thought they were doing up there. Didn't look like it was an ambush. Some local who never went heads-up with the Army decided he could block us I guess. He's sure not going to try it twice.

The whole damn column grinds to a halt about a mile short of the gap. Twenty thousand guys backed up halfway to the Elbe, leaning on their shields, tapping their pila, chomping a sausage roll... Cavalry trotting back and forth on the flanks eyeing the bushes for bandits.

I'm about fifty feet from Caesar. Steam coming out his ears. He's on foot like always. He leans down to the Prefect Annullinus on his horse and says, 'Prefect, take a detachment and clean that out'.

Annullinus heads for the rear and comes back soon enough with some of Flavia's battlegroup plus missile troops and artillery up the wazoo. They head straight for the gap in a cloud of dust.

I'm an old gunner, I can't resist this. Gods and Shades, I love the guns. I get leave to go with a scorpion section. The tribes are just standing there watching the show.

Sure enough there's marshy ground in the gap. The cavalry hits the base of the spur at the walk, then wheels west up the southward side, and halts. On their right, a cohort of infantry forms a column. Another deploys as force protection for the archers and batteries, and another forms up a few hundred feet west in a gully up the side of the ridge. Some more infanteers and missile troops go past the rear of the cavalry at the quickstep and set up on the far side.

I go with the north side batteries. I got to tell you, I never seen engines handled like that in my life. The infantry throw up a screen in front, the archers start with a harrassing fire to discourage local initiative, the scorpions set up practically arm-to-arm behind the force protection all around the base of the spur, and when the force on the south gets into position the Prefect blows the order and every engine lets go at once.

The section optios quit calling salvos after about four, it's shoot as you will and they just rip everything right off the top of that spur. I don't think I counted to five hundred before the trumpets blow again and the horse and foot start heading up the hill, and the force in the gully goes up to take them in flank. We shift aim a little and then they're past us, and from the rear I hear trumpets and the main column is on the move over the base of the spur, hell bent for leather down the road to Mainz.

I don't think the whole thing took an hour. I don't think we took twenty casualties. The infanteers never even deployed out of column. But by the Bull's Horns did we ever kill bandits.

Chapter Seven

After the Surge Was Over:
A Revolt in Libya

Our history now descends from a kingdom of gold to one of iron and rust.

—Dio Cassius[1]

As this is written, Canada has just closed out a twelve-year combat commitment in Afghanistan. The question *Was it worth it?* is being debated in public, and no doubt will be for years to come, and now we are in the Middle East. What we have seen in the previous chapter provides a counterpoint from an episode in history when the book has long been closed and the last echoes died away seventeen hundred years ago. We can allow ourselves to inspect the long view, the intermediate view, and the immediate short-term view.

In the long term, as we now know, 'Rome fell'. More specifically, in 260—twenty-five years after the surge into Germany—the Upper Rhine frontier was swamped by the Alemanni, and the Ten Cantons in the south were lost permanently. Hard fighting stabilized the

---

[1] Written about events after Marcus Aurelius' death. Dio didn't live to see how bad things really got.

theatre but it remained under intermittent threat through the fourth century. In 406 the depleted garrison of the Rhine—if there was any significant force left there at all by then—was overrun, and thereafter Roman power in the West was taken apart piecemeal.

If we ask the question from that long a perspective, the conclusion might be that Julius Caesar shouldn't have bothered in the first place. But that begs John Maynard Keynes' famous response: in the long run we are all dead.

From the medium-term point of view, the operation stabilized the Roman frontier from Regensburg[2] to the mouth of the Rhine for the next twenty-five years. That may not seem like much from this end of the telescope, but to the people who lived and raised kids and crops in that part of the Empire it probably felt very much worth it. How many parts of Europe before 1815 knew a generation's peace? (To look at these three perspectives does not tell us anything at all about what conclusions might be drawn from equivalent views of, say, Afghanistan.)

The short term is the most interesting—and the most immediately disastrous—outcome. The Emperor himself didn't survive it.

Maximinus Thrax ruled from early 235 to the middle of 238 CE. As we have seen in the last chapter, he was a

---

[2] *Castra Regina*, base of *III Italica* and the western anchor of the Upper Danube theatre.

giant of a man, allegedly[3] the first legionary ever to discover a marshal's baton in his knapsack. The primary sources say he was a barbarian (that is, from beyond the frontier, but inner-Empire writers like Herodian found it difficult to distinguish frontier ethnicity in practice and, as we shall see, had every reason to denigrate him after his death). Thrax—as his name implies—was more likely a Thracian from the east Balkans, of the same ethnic origin as Spartacus the gladiator three centuries before.

Maximinus Thrax 'Victor over Germany'
235-238 CE. Mr. Roger Lucy

By 235 he was a general with a distinguished record, but he seems to have been as rude, crude, and lewd as

---

[3] This also may not be true, but if he joined under Septimius Severus (193-211) there is no real need to discount it either. Promotion was becoming more open and once you made centurion (and, by Severus' legislation, thereby got your gold ring of equestrian status) there was no real limit. His birth would not have been a very relevant selection criterion to the generals who decided on him as best available candidate in the putsch of 235.

the day he joined. He was a very large, tall man with strong features (and big feet: in the next century very large men were nicknamed "Maximinus' boot").[4] He must have been something to see at mess dinners, and as our off-the-record source noted in the previous chapter, could probably talk nearly eye-to-eye with someone sitting on a cavalry horse.

A putsch on the Rhine had made him Emperor in 235. He spent the next two years hammering the Germans and some of the middle Danube tribes. He faced two major problems, one political and personal, the other economic and structural.

Maximinus was not the first Emperor who never visited Rome. That honour belongs to the short-lived Emperor Macrinus (217-218), who was acclaimed in the East and never left it. Even in the space of a year he had had trouble with the City populace as a result. By the next century Rome wasn't even a capital city, but nobody could have known at the time that the absentee Emperor was a sign of things to come.

What Maximinus entirely failed to grasp was that there was a personal and political relationship between the Emperor and the City unlike any other in the Empire.[5] Well, it was *their* Empire (and Emperor) as far as they were concerned.

---

[4] This tidbit comes to us from the *Historia Augusta* via *A Chronicle of the Roman Emperors* by Chris Scarre, 1995.

[5] David Potter in *The Roman Empire at Bay* (second edition 2014) persuasively analyzes the diverse constituencies with which the Emperors had to deal.

He seems to have gone through some of the motions. According to the *Historia Augusta* he sent pictures of his German victory to the Senate and People with an enthusiastic (and apparently self-dictated) dispatch:

> *And when he had thus conquered Germany, he despatched a letter, written to dictation, to the senate and people at Rome, the purport of which was this: "We cannot, Conscript Fathers, tell you all that we have done. Throughout an area of forty or fifty miles we have burned the villages of the Germans, driven off their flocks, carried away captives, killed men in arms, and fought a battle in a swamp. And we should have pushed on to the forests, had not the depth of the swamps prevented our crossing." Aelius Cordus says that this oration was entirely his own; and it is easily believed. For what is there in it of which a barbarian soldier were not capable? He wrote likewise to the people, to the same effect but with greater respect, this because of his hatred of the senate, by which, he believed, he was mightily despised. He gave orders, furthermore, for pictures to be painted and hung up before the Senate-house, illustrating the conduct of the war, in order that the art of painting, too, might tell of his exploits. But after his death the senate caused these pictures to be taken down and burned.*[6]

---

[6] Herodian reports there was such a dispatch and paintings. For what it may be worth, the *Historia Augusta* claims that this was it.

The economic and structural factors were more important. Surges cost money, a lot of it, as anyone in the Congressional Budget Office will confirm. Alexander had wanted to try paying off the Alemanni, which might indeed have been cheaper (and his finance officials may have made the point to him), but with the Persian theatre still unresolved and a large and restive army at Mainz, that was not going to happen. Putsches also cost money, and Maximinus had to pay 'bonuses' out of ready cash to the troops. On top of which, however many cattle there were in Germany to be used as provisions, the campaign was not going to be self-financing either. And Maximinus compounded matters by spending 236-237 campaigning on the Danube.

There is one, often overlooked, very important difference between the Roman Empire and any modern state. The Imperial government was cash-and-carry all the way. There was no national debt, nor even the remotest concept of one. If you didn't have it, you couldn't spend it. That simple fact (usually manifest in unpaid bonuses to the troops) cost more than one Emperor his life.[7] By about 300 they were getting close to the idea of a national *budget* for taxation purposes, but that was as far as Imperial fiscal policy development ever got.

Decent Emperors tried very hard. Debasing the silver currency was the usual expedient and up to the late second century there had been a lot less of this than you

---

[7] In the second century, an affluent government had instituted something very like a family allowance scheme for orphans (the *alimenta*). By the early third, it was cut back until it disappeared. The Christian Church seems to have filled some of the vacuum.

might think.[8] Watering silver is less easy than running the printing presses, and it was even harder to water gold because the prime users—the Army, the peoples beyond the frontier who were getting 'foreign aid', and the luxury traders in Sri Lanka[9]—knew bad money when they saw it.

---

[8] The silver *denarius* (a *denarius* was the most common silver coin, a *sestertius* or sesterce was also a coin but more importantly was the standard accounting unit) was remarkably stable between 90%-98% fineness until 117. It dipped a little lower during Trajan's invasion of Parthia, then drifted slowly down to 74% by the end of Commodus' reign in 192. After that it was kitty bar the door—45% by 235, then over the edge until by about 260, Roman domestic currency was worthless for over fifty years.

The gold coinage did decline in weight but not purity, and slowly enough not to matter significantly. However as early as the fifth century, conspiracy theories were loose that Constantine (d. 337) had converted to Christianity just to liquidate the precious metals frozen in pagan temples. This is unlikely.

[9] Ceylon = *Taprobane*. Pliny the Elder in the first century CE is the first commentator in history to complain about balance of payments deficits. He estimated grumpily: *By the lowest reckoning, India, Seres (China) and the Arabian peninsula take from our Empire 100 millions of sesterces every year: that is how much our luxuries and women cost us.* — Pliny the Elder, *Natural History* 12.84.

For a first-hand survey of the trade in Pliny's time, see the *Periplus Maris Erythraei* (colloquially translated: *Navigators' Guide to the Red Sea*), available in good translations with commentary. For the Romans, the 'Red Sea' meant anything eastward to India. Wikipedia has a useful map of all the places it mentions under the entries 'Periplus of the Erythraean Sea' and 'Sino-Roman Relations'. Imperial traders went breathtakingly far in search of a sesterce.

In 166 Marcus Aurelius almost invented the Victory Bond. The financial strains of his war with the Marcomanni were so pressing that he auctioned off the Palace valuables in the Forum. When the annual revenues came in and the government was solvent again, he bought them back from anyone who wanted to sell. (No mention of interest rate is made in the sources.)

Too many financially desperate Emperors simply confiscated. Nero didn't water the currency much but he managed to thin out the landowning class of North Africa (Tunisia) so badly that for the rest of history as much as half of the land was in Imperial estates.

Maximinus was a general, put in power by other generals, mainly in response to what they seem to have seen as an urgent need for firmer military leadership.[10] There is no reason to think he had any more acquaintance with or sympathy for civilian life than a brief visit or two to Italy as a private citizen—if indeed he had ever visited at all—would have given him. His concern was for the corporate interests of the Army first and—probably a long way second—Imperial defence writ large.

His only real concern for the Empire was how much ready cash it could produce for the Army. He was so oblivious to everything else that he didn't even bother to replace most of Alexander's senior provincial officials,

---

[10] There really is no way of reconstructing the politics behind the 235 putsch, except that they were probably more complex than the sources suggest. Then again, it may have been no more than senior officers' panic at Alexander's sudden decision to negotiate, with a large and restive army already concentrated.

except for the financial procurators who could get him the money. By 237 at latest, taxes were crushing and treason trials and confiscations were in full swing.

Then he cut the social safety net.

Rome was the biggest city in the known world at the time (possibly 1.2 million; Chang'an in Han China may have been as great) and it was not anywhere near economically self-sustaining. The urban proletariat depended almost entirely on the in-kind welfare system of grain and other foodstuffs (the *annona*) that had come into existence in the last century of the Republic and never stopped growing until the fifth century.[11] Lowering the welfare payments threatened starvation. Exactions in the provinces broadened unrest.

Even the Army was not that happy; Maximinus seems to have been playing favourites among the units. He also seems to have forgotten that soldiers have relatives. The Praetorian Guard and *II Parthica*, who were with him in theatre, were based in Rome, had relatives directly affected by the cuts, and were getting nasty letters from home by the basketful.

By March 238 the pot was boiling. The Emperor was in headquarters at Sirmium[12] on the Danube when the lid blew off in one of the more unlikely places, the province of Proconsular Africa, the modern Tunisia, one of the

---

[11] By now it also included salt and olive oil. Aurelian around 274 changed the format to baked bread (less fire hazard) and added pork (agricultural production subsidy?), at which point an exasperated official is said to have cried, 'What, we'll be giving them live geese and chickens next!'

[12] Srmska Mitrovica in Serbia.

most productive and densely settled regions of North Africa, which had no garrison at all and whose Governor, a Senator named Marcus Antonius (?) Gordianus Sempronianus Romanus was about eighty-two years old. His name alone tells how respectable he was, even if none of the sources can agree on just who he was related to; they all agree his family tree went back a long way—in his case, personally.

He was Governor at Carthage, and presumably not much interested in real governing, the more so as he was an Alexander Severus legacy and would have been staying well under the radar of the new regime. His nominal subordinate the Procurator was another and altogether nastier kettle of fish. He was a Maximinus appointee. He set about raising funds to meet Maximinus' requisition, and he threatened to ruin the landowning class—Roman Africa was a very prosperous place—with his exactions. Eventually things came to a head, and the sons of the nobility got together, armed their peasants with the archetypal shovels, rakes, and implements of destruction, and assassinated the Procurator in a small town called Thysdrus.[13] Herodian tells the story *con brio*:

> *The procurator of Africa was a man who performed his duties with excessive severity; he handed down extremely harsh decisions and extorted money to win the emperor's favor. Maximinus always appointed men who subscribed to his way of thinking. The treasury officials*

---

[13] El Djem in Tunisia

at that time, even if they happened to be honest, which was rarely the case, since they foresaw their own risks and knew the emperor's avarice, acted as dishonestly as the rest, even if they did so against their will.

Then the procurator of Africa, who acted the tyrant with everyone, involved in lawsuits some young men of the wealthiest and most aristocratic local families and undertook to extort money from them and rob them of their inheritances. Angered by this, the youths promised to pay him the money, but requested a delay of a few days. Calling a meeting, they won the support of all who were known to have suffered an injury or feared that they might suffer one. They ordered the field laborers to come into the city at night armed with clubs and axes.

Obeying their masters' orders, the workmen entered the city in a body before daybreak, carrying arms for hand-to-hand fighting hidden under their clothes. A large number assembled; for Africa, which is a heavily populated province, has many farmers.

When dawn was approaching, the youths appeared and ordered the mob of workmen to follow them as if they were simply part of the crowd; they directed the workmen to take their assigned positions and, keeping their weapons hidden, to resist bravely if any of the soldiers or the people should attack them to avenge the deed they were plotting.

Carrying daggers under their robes, the youths approached the procurator as if to discuss the payment of the money; then, attacking him suddenly, they stabbed and killed him. When his bodyguards drew their swords in retaliation, the workmen from the fields pulled out their clubs and axes and, fighting for their masters, easily routed their opponents.

Then the young Africans faced the classic question that bedevils every revolution the morning after: *Uh—What do we do now, guys???* Being stuck for an answer, they went to Governor Gordian, who was in town at the time, and offered him the Purple. Apparently they did it with conviction: *accept the offer and Maximinus might kill you later, but we'll do it right now if you don't.*

Sources differ as to whether he was horrified or flattered (Herodian plumps for both), but he took the offer and the surname Africanus and promptly associated his son, also Marcus Antonius (?) Gordianus Sempronianus Romanus Africanus and now to be known as Gordian II, in the Emperor's office.

Gordian Senior went up to the provincial capital of Carthage and wrote to the Senate at Rome telling them that there was a new claimant in Africa. The delegation of officers that carried the dispatch was also ordered to kill Maximinus' Praetorian Prefect in Rome, Vitalianus, which they did. The Senate promptly recognized them as legitimate rulers and outlawed Maximinus Thrax, pulled down his statues, and purged anyone they could find who was too prominently identified with the regime.

Everyone was overlooking one thing. Apart from the aforesaid peasants, farm implements, and some detached-duty centurions, the revolutionaries in Africa had no armed force at all. Maximinus seems to have grasped the point. He also seems not to have panicked. Herodian says that he waited two days after the news from Rome hit town[14] before he assembled the army and said, among other things:

> But the fact is (and you will have to laugh when you hear it) that the Carthaginians have taken leave of their senses and have either persuaded or compelled a miserable old man, doddering in advanced senility, to accept the throne, making sport of the empire as if in deliberate mockery. In what army do they trust, these men among whom lictors are sufficient to protect the proconsul? What kind of weapons do they carry, these men who have no arms except the spears they use in single combat with animals? Dancing, sarcastic quips, and rhythmic posturing[15] are their methods of training for war.

[14] He did fly into a screaming-and-throwing-things rage before getting outrageously drunk for a day and a night. Apparently nobody really wanted to be around him after that but, as with the nastier dictators of today, he had his ways of keeping the team together.

[15] We can guess that these phrases constitute the ancient derogatory equivalent of 'square-bashing'. Parade-square drill as we know it was invented by the Prussians in the 18th century, but the Romans had something of the concept. 'Dances' occurs regularly in Roman and Byzantine contexts where we would say 'marches'. The film *Zulu* (1964) gives a superb depiction of how drill can appear in a trained non-modern-European military.

He then set out for Rome with most of his expeditionary force and a large number of the Germans he had recruited in the surge two and a half years before.

Meanwhile in Africa the situation went south in a hurry. In the next-door province of Numidia[16] to the west, Governor Capellianus, a Maximinus appointee, had two things going for him—one major personal grudge against the Gordians arising from a lawsuit, and one legion of regulars, *III Augusta*, based at Lambaesis[17] and the only significant armed force between Alexandria and the Strait of Gibraltar. Capellianus mobilized the legion and headed straight for Carthage, where he wiped out Gordian II and an enthusiastic mob of civilians just outside the city gates inside of an hour. Gordian I then hanged himself by his Imperial belt.[18] The *attentat* had lasted six weeks.

This put the Senate in something of a position. They had already sent dispatches to all of the provinces calling for revolution, but they would have no idea of the response for weeks or months.[19] Their stalking horse was out of play and they had a very large and angry Thracian coming down at them from the Danube with an army of real troops. Nominally there was a Rome garrison—the Praetorian Guard in Rome itself and *II Parthica* stationed at Albanum just northward—but most of their strength

---

[16] Algeria.

[17] Modern Lambessa.

[18] This was not, however, the origin of the Gordian Knot.

[19] In the end, most of the Empire supported the Senate, but Maximinus was between Rome and any possible help.

was in theatre under Maximinus' control and bearing down along with him. In the end, they would be his undoing.

Then a miracle happened. The Senate actually got its act together for the first time in a century or two and began some very methodical organizing. This may not be quite the surprise we have tended to think it was. By 238 many of the senior Senators would have been retired generals with field experience and some idea how to run a campaign even against bad odds. They had already nominated a Board of Twenty to administer the war effort for the Gordians. Now they elected two of the Board, Balbinus and Pupienus, as Emperors, declared Maximinus a public enemy (again), and began praying/drinking heavily. Two others of the Board, Tullius Menophilus and Rutilius (?) Crispinus, were already in the north trying to get a defence together.

Pupienus was a very experienced military man; Balbinus a very experienced civilian administrator. It seemed an ideal combination, but they didn't get along, and the rumour was that they were both compromise choices. The Republic had had moments like this, but it had been a while since then.

A second miracle happened. Maximinus came down like the wolf on the fold on the city of Aquileia, at the head of the Adriatic not far from where Trieste now is. The Aquileians shut their gates and prepared to resist to the death with organizational and logistics help from Crispinus and Menophilus, and Pupienus went north to help them out with whatever he could scrape together from the Praetorians not in theatre, the City Cohorts, the

Fire Brigade, and a German bodyguard he had picked up at some point in his career.

In Rome the populace revolted. They had no use for any of Balbinus, Pupienus, or the Senate itself, while apparently the Gordians had been well-known and popular while they were living in Rome. The citizens began rioting, and got into a running fight with the over-age Praetorians who had been left behind when Pupienus went north.

'Permanent Security'; a coin issued by Gordian III. One of the vainer hopes ever expressed on a Roman coin. Collection of Mr. Roger Lucy.

The fight appears to have been a highly destructive stalemate. Urban warfare then was even more a leveller between pros and amateurs than it is now. Troops in a big city with narrow streets, tall buildings, and heavy roof tiles were at a severe disadvantage. The ultimate resort was to burn the place to the ground, which seems to have happened here (a bit less than half of Rome was destroyed). The Praetorians apparently surrendered in their camp after the water was cut off.

The people demanded that the Emperor be none other than the thirteen-year-old grandson of Gordian I, Marcus Antonius (?) Gordianus Sempronianus Romanus. The Senate caved in and Gordian, now known as Gordian III, was duly sworn in.

The Aquileians held. At any rate they held out long enough for hunger to set in in Maximinus' army—he had set out without logistics again[20]—and for *II Parthica* to remember their wives and kids at Albanum. Apparently *Parthica* took the initiative, killed Maximinus, and established 'cool but correct' relations with the cityfolk, who set up a market for them safely outside the walls. Pupienus sent everyone back to their bases, and headed back to Rome with a small guard.

That should have been the end of it. It wasn't. By then he and Balbinus were no longer on speaking terms, the people were in tumult, and finally in June 238 the Praetorian Guard swarmed the Palace and terminated both of their reigns with extreme prejudice. Gordian III was then acclaimed sole Emperor and lasted for six years with help from assorted regents, one of whom—Philip the Arab— finally eliminated him during a campaign against the Persians in 244.[21]

At this point we enter the nasty, brutish, and long period known as 'the Barracks Emperors', and history

---

[20] The first large city he had encountered, Emona (Ljubljana), had simply evacuated its people and supplies in front of him.

[21] We think. That is the story as told by Roman sources including Ammianus who is usually reliable. Persian sources insist that he was killed by them in a battle that Roman historians do not acknowledge (the same Persian inscription boasts of capturing large numbers of Germans, many of whom must have originally been recruited during the surge of 235). Philip himself always claimed that Gordian had died of natural causes.

draws a discreet veil over the shambles.[22] What emerged on the other end of almost fifty years of darkness was another kind of Roman Empire entirely.

---

[22] In this case literally. 'The Barracks Emperors' is usually described as the period 235-285, from the accession of Maximinus to the accession of Diocletian. But the sources for 235-238 are ample compared to what comes after. The history of the rest of the period is nearly impossible to reconstruct with any accuracy.

Chapter Eight

Perception's Mirror:
Defining Empire

Any ambitious Goth wants to be like a Roman. Only a very poor Roman would want to be like a Goth.

—*Theoderic the Ostrogoth, ruler of Italy 493-526*

After about sixty years out of fashion except as an epithet, the concept of 'empire' is making an intellectual comeback. Its latest incarnation almost always applies to the Americans, usually couched in phrases like 'the Decline and Fall of the American Empire'. There is debate in the commentariat as to whether or not America is or ever was an empire, and if so, whether it is truly declining and falling.

A recent Canadian contribution, *Enduring Empire* from University of Toronto Press (2009), explores the concept of American empire by drawing threads between modern Washington and ancient Athens and Rome. It is an edited collection by political and historical theorists and it sheds some light, direct and indirect, on the difficulties of defining 'empire'.

Oddly it never quite manages to arrive at a satisfactory definition of empire itself, though the collection offers some major insights into both ancient societies.

It needs definition, and the book's choice of historical ground throws the need into stark relief. Without a set of definitions ('qualifying standards') for 'empire', the collection goes astray from the beginning by including Periclean Athens as one of its two comparative cases in classical history. The essayists have many interesting points to make about Athens' political dynamic. Yet Periclean Athens, though colloquially called an empire, isn't all that convincing against any consistent yardstick.

Ever since the Romans coined the word *imperium* (literally, a legally mandated command power, not originally territorial), the Roman Empire has been the touchstone for everything large, powerful, impressive, brutal, overwhelming, overweening, and even majestic. The English word is also applied colloquially to anything large, powerful, and corporate. The important word here is 'colloquial'.

The other important word is 'anachronism'. Vergil's *'imperium sine fine'* equates to our Canadian (originally Biblical) 'Dominion from Sea to Sea' but means nothing at all in terms of political science. The concept of empire in all its plumage did not come along until well after the loss of the Roman provinces in the West. The early Emperors were *princeps* ('first citizen'), *augustus* ('revered'), *imperator* ('commander') in assorted combinations; their domain was still the *res publica populi romani* ('Commonwealth of the Roman People').

After about the fourth century this gradually elided into *imperium* as the created and by then nostalgic mythos of late Rome took hold. But the phrase *Empire of the Romans* first shows up in a legal document only in 813 CE when the chancery of the Eastern Roman (which we call 'Byzantine') Emperor Michael I in Constantinople recognized Charlemagne as *Emperor of the Franks* after about thirteen years of bad East–West relations. (It hadn't helped that when Charlemagne was crowned 'Emperor of the Romans' by Pope Leo III, the Roman Emperor in Constantinople had happened to be a woman, Irene.) For the first time ever, 'empire' acquired a plural.

The English word is a colloquialism, not a legal or diplomatic term, and we need to pare things down for it to be useful in any political taxonomy. We can immediately exclude any entity that claims Mickey Mouse as a major territory. This eliminates any business 'empire', and anything to do with Big Commodity. Large private interests may influence or impact empires (viz: British Petroleum in any of several phases of its existence), or they may be used as instruments of sovereign power projection by imperial entities (viz Russian oligarchs and Chinese state-owned enterprises) but they are not 'empires'.

We also have to get rid of some emotional baggage. 'Empire' and the terms associated with it have always been semantically loaded, positively, negatively, or both at once. *'Pax Americana'* is never used these days except as a pejorative.[1] But Vergil meant 'the immense majesty of the Roman Peace' only positively, and after twenty years of unrestrained civil war he had every right to. A

---

[1] *'Pax Britannica'* could cut both ways; 'The Brutish Empire' had currency among Victorian liberals, as I believe Desmond Morris has noted.

century later Cornelius Tacitus wasn't so sure: 'They create a desolation and call it peace' are the words he puts in the mouth of a Caledonian chieftain. He may have been the first literary ancestor of Noam Chomsky, and if that is true then he has much to answer for indeed.

Niccolo Macchiavelli was the first theoretician of 'empire'. Edward Gibbon contributed the concept that empires rise, decline, and fall in one smooth curve and that this is the result of moral deficiency ('the triumph of barbarism and religion').[2] But any empire worth its salt has many ups and downs, because it has many centuries over which to experience them, and morality has nothing to do with it. Third-century Romans were as puritan as they come,[3] and they lived through a period that may have held more concentrated disaster than some phases of the Fall of the West two centuries after.

It is no help that throughout history, many states have been called empires that shouldn't be. It's acceptable to call states that existed before Rome 'empires' provided that they meet the qualifying standards (e.g., Assyria, Persia—but nobody calls Pharaonic Egypt an 'empire'), but many people since Rome's fall have called themselves Emperors who couldn't have claimed a cheap

---

[2] American historian Chester G. Starr has commented that thanks to Gibbon 'what most people know about the Roman Empire is that it declined and fell'.

[3] They never really had orgies—Caligula, Nero, and later debauched Emperors like Commodus and Elagabalus were outliers and the upper classes despised them for it.

seat in the Colosseum. Objectively the Central African Empire (now the even more desperately-off Central African Republic) was not an empire except in someone's twisted mind.

Japan is more interesting. There's not much sovereign territory there, but 'Emperor' is a pretty eclectic translation of *'Mikado'* or *'Tenno'*. The Japanese have always thought of themselves as an 'imperial' sovereignty, mainly to keep up with the Son of Heaven over to the west; the chancery of Michael I would have understood. Things in that part of the world don't seem to be changing appreciably, with or without a Son of Heaven on the throne of the Middle Kingdom. Interestingly this sort of competitive pressure was just what Rome lacked for most of antiquity. They didn't have to call themselves an 'Empire'; they had no perceived equals on earth except the Parthian or Persian power out east. The Parthians by and large couldn't compete in status. The Persians made the competition ideological, and just about then (in the fourth century) Roman intellectuals started talking about 'empire'.

What makes an empire, then? How does a nation qualify for Tier One in the Geopolitical League?

An empire is a superpower. One of the reasons that the term 'empire' is once again attracting interest may well be that the post–World War II concept of 'one state, one vote' that embodied the United Nations is imploding. Even when two superpowers contended in the Cold War, there was a kind of doublethink going on that considered them to be just like any other state (only nuclear), and the centre of two allied power blocs. (Well, *we* were the Free World, *they* were the Evil Empire, but that merely illustrates how subjective this kind of taxonomy is.) In fact if there was an acknowledged hierarchy in the pre-1991 international system, it was between nuclear and non-nuclear states.

For about twenty years after the end of the Cold War around 1991, the international power structure remained in a kind of stasis, 'running on momentum'. That began to end after 2005, definitely signalled by Russia's attack on Georgia in August 2008. The 'post-post-Cold War multiverse' consists of around 193 members of the United Nations plus assorted other half-state, non-state, and failed-state actors, of which one (the Islamic State, otherwise known as ISIS/ISIL/IS) is becoming a serious regional threat. Middle Eastern politics in particular are becoming violently gridlocked as regional powers contend and US influence wanes. Eastern Europe may follow. How many and which states emerge as global powers is very unclear.[4]

In other words the international system is again sorting itself out into a hierarchy of power, and nomenclature is evolving to match. If 'empire' stays in fashion, which it may do only in journalistic argot, it will

---

[4] An interesting sidebar to this is the evolution of ad hoc, semi-permanent, sometimes-overlapping international groupings based on non-universal interests—G8 (in 2014 about to revert to G7?), G20, SCO, CSTO, NATO, and presumably more to come—in place of the universalist and increasingly ineffectual United Nations. The Roman Empire, being self-sufficient, didn't worry about the ineffectuality of international institutions.

end up denoting the top tier of the hierarchy. Conceivably you could be a superpower without being an empire but it doesn't happen often.

On the other hand a polity can temporarily lose superpower status and then come back. 'Temporary' is a term best evaluated in hindsight. The Byzantine Empire suffered several major setbacks between 565 and 1071 CE and only the last was terminal.

Debating whether America is now 'in an end of the Roman Republic phase' or more like 'Imperial Rome just before the Fall' is entertaining but pointless; there are interesting points of similarity between both, but the political histories do not parallel each other more than superficially. Taxonomy of political entities isn't a predictive tool.[5] And it is becoming increasingly obvious that in a complex system, relative power is extremely situational.

An empire is diverse. It may not start that way but it has to end that way. In fourth-century Rome, diversity still mattered. Gaul (France) still kept its Celtic customs and

---

[5] When I originally wrote this essay in 2009, I suggested that the dynamic of stabilization in the new global order might not necessarily imply future massive shifts in boundaries as regional powers attain Imperial status. That turns out to be a much more dubious claim than might have been thought. But since every square inch of the globe is now claimed (however ineffectually) by a sovereignty, Imperial expansion in the classic sense is going to be a good deal more difficult for the empires of tomorrow—but that hypothesis is still seriously challenged by Russia and the Islamic State.

even its own measurements (leagues instead of miles) four centuries after Caesar. The American 'melting pot' is turning out to have more lumps in the soup than anyone imagined. Stalin's 'nationalist in form, socialist in substance' slogan was an attempt to square Marxism with Great Russian chauvinism.

Likewise the home territory of an empire becomes populated with every race and nationality in and around the empire; Juvenal was complaining loudly about this in the second century, but the influx of immigrants was (and usually is) for the better. This is one significant excluder for Athens as an empire—Athenians never permitted such dilutions.

Susan Mattern[6] contributes a very intriguing study of the ways, means, and practical extent of Roman power in conquered territory under the Republic. She notes that in nearly every studyable case, Rome had a deep and intricate web of pre-existing relationships before actual territorial annexation took place, and that however violent the actual conquests were, they were aided and supported by substantial portions of the population.[7] There is no reason to believe that the successful expansions that took place under the Empire were any different. Britain (and other European powers) tended to follow a similar pattern later. Russia and America expanded into perceived political vacuums, and had some unpleasant surprises where the space turned out to have occupants.

---

[6] *Enduring Empire.*

[7] Cicero comments that 'not a sesterce changes hands in Gaul but is entered in a Roman ledger'.

It seems worth suggesting that an empire has reached its limit of direct territorial rule when it runs into cultures which for various reasons it cannot assimilate because they have too little in common to begin with. Augustus was one of the sharpest political operators in history but it took ten years and the loss of three legions to make him realize that trans-Rhine Germany simply would not be assimilated. South Britain had close enough relations with Roman Gaul that it could both pose a perceived threat and be assimilated fairly easily; North Britain was another matter and seems to have resembled Afghanistan then or now (you don't keep fifteen thousand men in a controlled zone in the middle of nowhere for nearly three hundred years on Rome's constrained resources without a serious perceived need).

Repeated invasions of Parthia, massive and very costly, achieved nothing permanent and had a serious tendency to backfire.

An empire is universalist. An empire lasts because it gives the conquered something worth having, even if by imposition—legal system, governance, taxation system, culture, at the very least some basic sort of protection and order. (Niall Ferguson has tried to distinguish between 'good' and 'bad' empires, but most leave a very mixed heritage. Responses even in Russia itself to Putin's attempted *reconquista* are less than wholly enthusiastic, but the USSR did at least keep the peace within its borders.)

Universalism can be praiseworthy or indictable depending on your point of view. The famous 'What have the Romans ever done for us?' scene in *Monty Python's Life of Brian* is pretty close to a straight lift from the *Babylonian Talmud*:

> *Why did they call [Rabbi Judah ben Ilia] the first of the speakers? For once Rabbi Judah and Rabbi Jose and Rabbi Simeon were sitting, and Judah son of proselytes was sitting with them. Rabbi Judah began and said: "How excellent are the deeds of this nation. They have instituted market places, they have instituted bridges, they have instituted baths." Rabbi Jose was silent. Rabbi Simeon ben Yohai answered and said: "All that they have instituted they have instituted only for their own needs. They have instituted market places to place harlots in them; baths, for their own pleasure; bridges, to collect toll." Judah son of proselytes went and reported their words and they were heard by the government. They said: "Judah who exalted shall be exalted; Jose who remained silent shall be banished to Sopphoris; Simeon who reproached shall be put to death."* [8]

---

[8] *Babylonian Talmud*, Sabbath 33b, excerpted by Lewis and Reinholt, *Roman Civilization Sourcebook II, The Empire*, 1955. Rabbi Simeon spent the next fourteen years hiding out in a cave, but they never caught him. The argument evokes the 'sure the West has a great consumer economy but they bomb wedding parties' line of modern political discourse.

The rule seems to be, universal where it counts, diverse where it's useful or not worth fighting over. Gaul kept its leagues but paid its taxes, and Gauls (and nearly everyone else) sat in the Senate by 200 CE. Official propaganda promoted 'commonwealth (*res publica*)' far earlier than 'empire'.

An empire has critical mass. It has territory, manpower, and resources on a scale entirely beyond all or most of its regional neighbours. Resilience is key. Already in the last half of the third century BCE, ruling only Italy, Rome could take incredible losses both on land and sea against Carthage and still make them good. Arthur Eckstein notes in *Enduring Empire* that the Roman Republic lost *ninety* major battles and *forty* commanding generals in the process of acquiring an empire. The curve is clearly not smooth.

By comparison, to *hold* an empire, the Imperial Army was no larger than about three hundred and fifty thousand men strung from Northumbria to Sinai, and Victorian Britain post-Crimea never had more than about eleven thousand men under arms abroad outside India.[9] But the resources were there when needed in both cases—to a point. The tipping point was when economic stress no longer permitted military recovery. The psychological tipping point was where the frontier could be successfully penetrated on a regular basis

---

[9] *Send a Gunboat! The Victorian Navy and Supremacy at Sea 1854-1904* (second edition, 2007) has many wise things to say about how Victorian England held power economically. The wisest Caesars used the same toolkit.

with relative impunity. There is no way that a few hundred thousand men can hold so long a frontier by brute force.

Most pre- and post-Roman empires have been geographically contiguous (e.g., China, Persia, Russia). There is one line of discussion that concerns itself with classifying empires on this basis (in some theorizations, an empire based on sea power becomes a *thalassocracy*). Rome was the first empire with 'a hole in the middle' (i.e., the Mediterranean) but even without much of a standing navy, as long as she controlled the whole coastline this was more an advantage than not given the huge benefits of sea transport on interior lines. Projecting power by land to some of the more distant frontiers was addressed by forward defence, but running a sustainable internal economy over long land distances proved much harder. Byzantine Rome was in a more difficult position, having strong rival naval forces to contend with at most points in her history.

In the modern age, Spain, Portugal, Britain, and Holland showed early on that a global empire can be held together, though probably Victorian Britain's near-monopoly of sea trade and manufacturing was more profitable to her than any part of the land empire except possibly India. The French and Germans had varying experiences in running overseas empires, but the Germans lost theirs through collapse at home, and the French dismantled gradually after World War II in common with all surviving European empires except Russia.

An empire is durable, in time and in memory. You don't qualify for empire status until you've matured to the point where it is impossible to imagine life without you.[10] Rome achieved superpower status when she finally defeated Hannibal in 202 BCE and held it until the Turks defeated her in 1071 CE, and, diminishingly, for about two generations after.

Rome's political legacy in Western Europe was a 'mythic hangover' that included the concept of empire itself. The sack of the City of Rome by Alaric the Goth in 410 probably exceeded 9/11 for popular impact, and for centuries afterward, people longed for the good old days. Saxon chieftains wore derivative Roman generals' uniforms (residents of the former Soviet Union will relate to this). The myth of Eternal Rome was powerful enough that in 800 Pope Leo III could declare a Holy Roman Empire (which, as Voltaire said, was none of the above) that lingered until Napoleon put it out of everyone's misery. The real, functioning, Roman Empire was still there in 800, headquartered in Constantinople and thoroughly unhappy with the Pope.

Perhaps more than anything else, lack of maturity is what disqualifies Periclean Athens as an empire,

---

[10] Finley in *Aspects of Antiquity* points out that no matter how bad we may think life in the fourth and fifth century Roman Empire may have been, nobody at the time could have proposed or envisaged an alternative. In 449 CE, a Greek merchant who had defected to the court of Attila the Hun tells the Roman envoy Priscus (more or less) that 'the institutions of the Romans are fair, it's the people who run them that are the problem'. This has a familiar ring.

followed by lack of scope. The Athenians had power for just eighty years, half of which they spent in a losing death-struggle with Sparta, and they never cared about their alleged empire except to ransack it for money. They had 'hegemony' (dominant influence) but not 'empire'.

One important variable distinguishing modern and classic concepts of empire is the tightening of the definition of sovereignty. Roman frontiers were less well-defined than the remains of fortifications make them look today, although by the first century CE they had a pretty clear idea of where the Empire ended and the sphere of influence began, which is something the Americans now appear to be learning. However the modern impulse to define territorial sovereignty very precisely makes the difference between power, influence, and hegemony rather more important. (Meanwhile the concept of 'ungoverned lands' is returning to contemporary vocabulary. A Roman or classical Chinese diplomat would have had no problem grasping it. Getting through those lands alive would be something else again. Check the monthly travel advisories as posted by the Logothete's Office in Constantinople. And go heavily armed.)

Although the French Empire had a relatively short run, it has had remarkable durability, by no means all negative, in the minds of post-colonial peoples (as of course has Britain with a longer run and broader reach in its time). When a successor state asks for help, and such requests recur and are answered over a period of decades, that means something. The 2013-14 French interventions in Mali and the Central African Republic are the latest example.[11]

An empire is acquired, not created. Generally you should not be aware that you are an empire until you already have the credibility. Napoleon and Hitler set out to create empires and were resisted and destroyed head-on. Alexander the Great is the great what-if of Western history. Genghis Khan and Timur are perhaps less 'what-if?' than 'what happened?' All three were unstoppable conquerors. All left a slew of successor states and cultural influences. None left a unified realm, and all three may have suffered the consequences of a too-rapid expansion, even without serious opponents. With the Islamic State it is a little early to tell.

(Attempts at territorial *reconquista* on an imperial scale are extremely rare and have no good track record. The East Roman Emperor Justinian tried over thirty years to reconquer a Western Empire that had taken centuries to create; he failed in the face of overwhelming economic and political stresses. Now Vladimir Putin of Russia seems to have similar ambitions. Given Russia's economic weakness and long-term political shakiness, his

---

[11] Just because they're respected doesn't mean they're always successful. The French attempt to help with the current humanitarian disaster in the Central African Republic hauntingly evokes Gildas' account of a plea for help of the mid-fifth century: 'To Aetius, a noble Roman, the groans of the Britons. The barbarians drive us to the sea, the sea drives us back to the barbarians'. The French at least are doing their best; Aetius never answered.

odds of success do not look good. Two examples hardly make a model but they are suggestive.)[12]

Rome had its core empire by 50 BCE, acquired in unplanned chunks. 'Manifest Destiny' was manufactured while Augustus was trying to clean up after the Civil Wars—but real imperial self-consciousness only emerged gradually when Rome was on the ropes after 250 CE, and it fostered the mythic hangover already mentioned.

Rudyard Kipling's tales and poems pose a wistful counterpoint to British imperial self-awareness in a time of fading, and late Victorian sensibilities cast a backward and romantic glow onto the 'Fall of Rome'. Kipling had a good intuition of 'how this ends'. He coined the phrase 'white man's burden', not as jingoist cant, but in the sense of 'Look what we've done to ourselves' and a solemn warning to the Americans not to do the same in the Philippines. The Roman intelligentsia of the fourth and fifth centuries also had a sense of fading greatness, and there was sharp acrimony even in a top-down political system. There were some familiar debates in the vein of concession vs. resistance.[13]

So, then, is America really an empire? By all the criteria cited here, it is an empire—but in that case it has been one since 1890, when the frontier officially closed. Arguably, the real American Empire is the forty-eight

---

[12] China can be argued as an exception. But for much of its history, China has been more of a cultural unity than a political one. The list of dynasties is deceptive.

[13] Synesius' *On Kingship* around 400 is a remnant of this dialogue.

continental states plus Alaska and Hawaii and a few island territories. It became one with perhaps more self-awareness of the process than the British or Romans had; it could hardly help it having their examples before it, but not with any grand design. What America consciously tried to become in the early twenty-first century is something else again. Late twentieth-century America had 'hegemony' beyond its imperial boundaries and influence far beyond hegemony. After 2001 there was a conscious effort to project hegemony and to remake the world in a certain image. At the moment both hegemony and influence are being heavily contested abroad and at home.

After 1945 there were two hegemons on Earth: Russia and the US. After 1989 there was one. There were always three empires counting China, but China has been in occlusion since about 1800. There are still three empires, and the other two are restoring their influence and reasserting their hegemonic ambitions. And there is an unknown number of possible other claimants, for the growth of empire is unpredictable.

America's hegemony now has rivals. But its 'empire' seems quite secure, at least from external threats. There is no immutable law that says that America's—or any other nation's—sovereign boundaries are forever inviolable, or that its domestic society and polity are not subject to lines of fracture. But, by and large, the omens do not seem evil.

Further Reading

An eclectic selection of sources, with which you should be able to explore as deeply as you wish.

The Web

The Web has accumulated a very deep vein of resources in classical history. As always, it should be approached with caution since much information on it is unverified. However, many of the Wikipedia entries on classical topics are well-furnished with citations, and it is an excellent repository of texts and translations of almost all of the major and many of the minor classical sources. One of the principal classical text sites is Lacus Curtius.

The Harzhorn battle is mainly published on-line and in German (Google Translate does a workmanlike job). There is now a fine new museum and visitors' centre at the site itself.

The Roman re-enactor sites can be fascinating; the Ermine Street Guard (UK) is among the best. Romanempire.net is a fine hobbyist aggregator site. Like all historical re-enactors, its contributors tend to idealize.

YouTube has a plethora of Roman history videos, most grossly over-sensationalized. One that is not is *Roman Soldiers to Be* (BBC 2001) in which a classics professor and an RAF officer take a squad of recruits out to the moors of

Yorkshire, resulting in some fascinating discoveries about how things really worked under field conditions. It is intermittently viewable on BBC's website.

Scholarly Journals

There are many journals of classical studies in all major European languages. In English, one of the best is the *Journal of Roman Studies* of the Society for the Promotion of Roman Studies in the UK. Articles from the Journal since 1931 are now downloadable in PDF format for a small charge each from either Cambridge Journals Online or JStor. Students may have free access through their learning institutions.

Ancient Authors

Almost all available in original and translation either in print or online.

Cicero, *Letters to His Friends*, Book Ten, Letter Thirty (the Galba letter)

Appian, *Roman History*. Mid-second century CE. A useful supplement to Galba.

Cornelius Tacitus, *Histories, Annals, Agricola, Germania*. Early second century CE.

Dio Cassius (or Cassius Dio), *Roman History*. From the foundation of Rome, but the most valuable part is Commodus (180) to Alexander Severus (about 229), much of which Dio witnessed.

Herodian, *History of the Empire from the Death of Marcus*. Herodian may have been a first-hand witness of some of the events of Maximinus' reign.

Frontinus, *Strategems*. Late first century.

Arrian, *Deployment against the Alani (Ektaxis)*. The only description of an Imperial deployment we have to go on. Made harder to interpret by being written in Greek, when the language of the Army was Latin, with no agreed lexicon of equivalents.

Ammianus Marcellinus, *Res Gestae (Roman History)*. Late fourth century. A soldier and one of the best Roman historians. In our context, the story of the great siege of Amida by the Persians in 359 at which he was present shouldn't be missed.

The *Historia Augusta (Lives of the Later Caesars)*. Mid-fourth century (?). A notorious farrago of fact and fiction, this one has to be handled with lead tongs. It is nearly all we have for far too much of the third century.

And of course *Vegetius, De Rei Militari (On Military Affairs)*. He too has to be handled carefully as a source for the Imperial period as he mixes various stages of evolution together in a sort of historical mashup, but as an organizational manual he's just fine. His earliest traceable edition dates to 450 CE in Constantinople and he has never been out of circulation since.

Modern Authors

General History

Margaret MacMillan, *The Uses and Abuses of History*, 2009. A brief and cautionary read.

Sir Lawrence Freedman, *Strategy: A History*, 2013. Begins with God. Covers everything.

Stephen Greenblatt, *The Swerve: How the World Became Modern*, 2011. The ancient publishing industry, and its Renaissance rediscovery.

Anthony Preston, *Send a Gunboat! The Victorian Navy and Supremacy at Sea, 1854-1904*, second edition 2007. Practical Imperialism as an art form.

Tom Standage, *The Writing on the Wall*, 2013. Social media from Pompeii to Pinterest.

David Tabachnik and Toivo Koivukoski, *Enduring Empire: Ancient Lessons for Global Politics*, 2009.

Essays

Peter Brown, *The World of Late Antiquity: AD 150–750*, 1989.

M. I. Finley, *Aspects of Antiquity: Discoveries and Controversies*, 1991.

Republic and Empire

N. J. E. Austin and B. Rankov, *Exploratio: Military & Political Intelligence in the Roman World from the Second Punic War to the Battle of Adrianople*, 1998. Did the Governors at Mainz or Antioch really have a filing cabinet marked 'Intelligence'?

M. C. Bishop and J. C. N. Coulston, *Roman Military Equipment from the Punic Wars to the Fall of Rome*, 2006. Meticulous, scholarly, informative, and readable.

Peter Connolly, *Greece and Rome at War*, 2006. Still the best illustrations in the business.

Michael Grant, *Army of the Caesars*, 1974. The Army in Imperial politics.

Lawrence Keppie, *The Making of the Roman Army: From Republic to Empire*, 1998. Sets the standard for late Republican organization and practice, and the evolution into the Imperial standing army.

Pat Southern and Karen Ramsey Dixon, *The Late Roman Army*, 1996. A solid overview of the late third century response to crisis and the Army's metamorphosis as a result.

Eric W. Marsden, *Greek and Roman Artillery*, 1969. A pioneering work to which re-enactors still pay homage.

Rob S. Rice, Simon Anglim, Phyllis Jestice, Scott Rusch, John Serrati, *Fighting Techniques of the Ancient World (3000 B.C. to 500 A.D.): Equipment, Combat Skills, and Tactics,* 2003. More of the best illustrations in the business, mainly by Connolly.

Chris Scarre, *A Chronicle of the Roman Emperors*, 1997. A handy biographical encyclopedia, lavishly illustrated.

H. H. Scullard, *From the Gracchi to Nero: A History of Rome 133 B.C. to A.D. 68*, 1959. A fine general history.

Ronald Syme, *The Roman Revolution*, 1939. A dense and thorough reappraisal of the Augustan political dynamic.

Graham Webster, *The Roman Imperial Army*, third edition 1994, first published 1969. Still the go-to starter text for Imperial military organization.

Peter S. Wells, *The Barbarians Speak: How the Conquered Peoples Shaped Roman Europe*, 2001.

C R Whittaker, *Rome and its Frontiers: The Dynamics of Empire*, 2004. Both Wells and Whittaker have more than a whiff of post-colonialist ideology, but fine surveys of a poorly understood aspect of the Imperial milieu.

The Third Century and After

Anthony Birley, *The African Emperor: Septimius Severus*, 1988. Doing much with little.

Arther Ferrill, *The Fall of the Roman Empire: The Military Explanation*, 1986. The title is almost misleading, as Ferrill explains how the Western Empire was lost after 378 mainly due to pure neglect and mismanagement of its armed forces.

Michael Grant, *The Climax of Rome: The Final Achievements of the Ancient World, AD 161-337*, 1974. A major survey of a poorly understood period. The military achievement, the climax of Classical art and literature, the evolution of a faith-based society.

H. M. D. Parker, *A History of the Roman World AD 138 to 337*, 1935. A fine, if now somewhat dated, introduction to the dark years of the Empire.

David S. Potter, *The Roman Empire at Bay, AD 180-395*, second edition 2014. A fine interdisciplinary synthesis of the political and social dynamics at work in the third century and after. He mines the early Christian sources for clues to secular history and is very strong on the poorly documented Parthian/Persian society and 'East-West relations'.

Timeline

BCE

The Republic

202 | Defeat of Carthage; Rome emerges as a superpower.

168 | Defeat of Macedonia; Roman supremacy in Asia.

92 | Sulla makes first contact with the Parthians at the Euphrates.

63 | Pompey defeats Mithridates and imposes an eastern settlement; Armenia aligns toward Rome.

55 | Caesar defeats the Suebi under Ariovistus and makes a demonstration in force across the Rhine. He appears to have established Roman control up to the Rhine from this time forward but details are vague.

53 | Crassus loses his life and eight legions against the Parthians at Carrhae.

44 | The Ides of March; Octavian returns to Rome to assume Caesar's legacy.

43 | The Battle of Mutina: S. Sulpicius Galba writes to Cicero the morning after (April 15).

38 | The German tribe of the Ubii migrate into the Roman Rhineland, encouraged by Marcus Agrippa. The city of Cologne is founded.

31 | Battle of Actium; Octavian defeats Antony and ends the Civil Wars.

The Empire

27 | In a series of omnibus bills passed by the Senate, the constitutional foundations of Empire are laid. Octavian becomes Augustus. The Imperial Army begins to take shape.

13 | Mainz is founded by Tiberius' brother Drusus as a major base on the Upper Rhine.

12 BCE-6 CE | Tiberius and Drusus advance to the Elbe, which is envisaged as a permanent frontier. Rome also advances to the line of the Danube throughout its length.

2 | Augustus negotiates the return of Crassus' Eagles from Parthia. Public opinion is surprised.

CE

6 | The Great Pannonian Revolt takes three years and fifteen legions to suppress. Panic in the City.

9 | Battle of the Teutoburger Wald at Kalkreise; Governor Varus of Germany destroyed with three legions by

Hermann the Liberator. Rome abandons trans-Rhine Germany.

14-16 | Massive retaliatory raids into Germany led by Germanicus Caesar; two Eagles recovered. Wars with the federation of the Marcomanni in southern Germany.

40s | Sporadic fighting against tribes on the right bank of the Rhine. The third of Varus' Eagles is recovered.

60/61 | Boudicca's rebellion in Britain. The Ninth Legion under Petilius Cerialis suffers a major disaster.

58-63 | Nero's Parthian/Armenian wars, culminating in a peaceful settlement.

69-70 | The Year of Three Emperors. Vespasian emerges on top. The Civilis Revolt in northern Gaul, resolved by Petilius Cerialis.

74-78 | Julius Frontinus is Governor of Britain, following which (presumably) he writes his military texts.

78-85 | Julius Agricola is Governor of Britain. He attempts the conquest of Caledonia. His expeditionary force includes the Ninth Legion, by then based at York.

82 | The Ninth Legion suffers a heavy night attack on the northern expedition and has to be rescued.

82-83 | Domitian briefly campaigns on the Rhine.

85-89 | Major war with Dacia on the Middle Danube; two legions lost. Agricola recalled from Britain and Romans pull back to the line of the later Hadrian's Wall. Permanent strategic pivot from Rhine to Danube; Rhine army reduced from eight to four legions, British from four to three. The annexation of the Ten Cantons (*Agri Decumates*) between upper Rhine and upper Danube shortens the frontier. The Rhine frontier becomes quiet for over a century.

95 | Julius Frontinus appointed Commissioner of Waterworks for the City of Rome.

114 | Trajan invades Parthia with about half the Army. The campaign rapidly becomes a quagmire.

117 | Jewish revolt throughout the East. Trajan declares victory and withdraws to Antioch, dying en route. Around this time, 'something' apparently happens to the Ninth Legion in Britain, which is later transferred to the continent. Hadrian withdraws to former frontiers in the East.

135 | Arrian, Governor of Cappadocia, leads his corps out against an incursion of Alanic heavy cavalry. He later publishes his deployment orders.

161-165 | Parthian War of Marcus Aurelius. The army brings back plague from Ctesiphon. War ends inconclusively.

166-180 | Marcomannic Wars on the Upper Danube; 'creeping professionalization' of the higher command structure begins. Rhine remains peaceful. Sometime late in this period, the Upper Rhine confederation of the Alemanni begins to form.

197 | Parthian War of Septimius Severus. Upper Mesopotamia annexed as two provinces.

213 | The Alamanni attack Upper Germany. Caracalla conducts retaliatory attacks.

217-218 | Caracalla assassinated as he begins campaign against Parthia. Inconclusive outcome under Macrinus.

224 | Parthian regime overthrown, replaced by Sassanian Persians.

231-233 | Alexander Severus campaigns unsuccessfully against Persia.

233 | Second Alemannic attack forces breakoff of Persian campaign.

234 | Alexander concentrates massive expeditionary force on Mainz.

235 | Alexander attempts negotiations with Alemanni; overthrown by officers' putsch. Replaced by Maximinus

Thrax who leads expeditionary force deep into Germany. Battle at the Harzhorn.

238 | Revolt in Africa. Gordians I and II recognized by the Senate, but promptly suppressed. Maximinus advances into Italy. Senate appoints Balbinus and Pupienus Emperors. Civil unrest forces them to appoint Gordian III as well. Maximinus bogs down in front of Aquileia and is killed by his own troops. Gordian reigns until 244 and is overthrown after unsuccessful war with Persia.

260 | The Empire reaches the nadir of its history. Valerian captured by Persian King of Kings Shapur. Alemanni swamp Upper Rhine defences and occupy the Ten Cantons permanently.

Acknowledgements

I acknowledge with deepest thanks the help of Col. Ed Rayment and Pat Hind White of the Royal Canadian Military Institute, who made the lectures possible; Dr. Eric McGeer, historian, Byzantinologist, Commonwealth War Graves Commissioner, fellow member of the RCMI; Roger Lucy, a sharer in the calling, who assisted with sources and illustrations and opened his collection of Roman coinage to me; Kieran McAuliffe, master cartographer and fellow RCMI member; Derwin Mak, Catherine Davis @hadrianasblog on Hadrian's Wall, all of whom beta-read the first drafts, and Dr. M. C. Bishop @perlineamvalli, military archaeologist extraordinaire, who helped with hints on some difficult bits. The Ermine Street Guard (UK), pioneering re-enactor unit, who furnished the Eagle images and the lovely action photo of a Roman gunnery team found on page 47, and Iguana's cheerful and capable editorial team headed up by Amanda Plyley.

Iguana Books
iguanabooks.com

If you enjoyed *Roman Spaces: Essays Around an Empire*...
Look for other books coming soon from Iguana Books! Visit our official website for updates as they happen.

http://iguanabooks.com/

You can also learn more about Eric S. Morse and his upcoming work on his author page.

http://ericmorse.iguanabooks.com/

If you're a writer...
Iguana Books is always looking for great new writers, in every genre. We produce primarily ebooks but, as you can see, we do the occasional print book as well. Visit us at iguanabooks.com to see what Iguana Books has to offer both emerging and established authors.

http://iguanabooks.com/publishing-with-iguana/

If you're looking for another good book...
All Iguana Books works are available from our bookstore. We pride ourselves on making sure that every Iguana book is a great read.

http://iguanabooks.com/bookstore/

Visit our bookstore today and support your favourite author.

IGUANA